To The Point

the knitted triangle

quince&co.

Quince & Co
quinceandco.com

ISBN 978-0-9979187-3-1

Printed in the United States.

Contents

INTRODUCTION

Why the knitted triangle?

Triangular shawls have always been my favorite knitting projects. There's something soothing about the structure of it—a three-sided canvas, shaped along the edges through its entirety, with infinite possibility in how to fill the space of its interior—that makes shawl design irresistible to me.

A multitude of approaches on *how* to knit a triangle—whether they begin from the top or bottom, or are shaped by increases or decreases—are covered in this book by chapter, beginning with a good, all-around basic: Traditional top down, increasing triangles. They begin at the center of the top edge and steadily increase in size by adding stitches to the sides and center spine, ending with a long, bound off edge that forms the remaining two sides of the triangle.

From there, we move on to how modifying the rate of shaping can change a triangle's dimensions; then comes top-down, *decreasing* triangles, where the maximum number of stitches are cast on and decreased steadily down to a singular point. Next, bottom up triangles are covered, and the various approaches to that method of construction; and finally, to sideways knitted triangles, in a league of their own.

Triangular shawl design has come a long way since I first took up knitting, with clever short row techniques, modular knitting, and other wonderful construction methods and design elements being explored every day.

None of the patterns in this book are intended to reinvent the wheel: All of these pieces were born of the longing for something sweet, simple, and to the point.

THREE SIDES TO EVERY STORY

In the time since I began knitting nearly fifteen years ago, shawl construction has come a long way. Half-Pi, crescent, trapezoid, bias-knit parallelogram, boomerang—you name it, the most interesting shapes have come about from many a curious designer's mind, armed with innovative ways of utilizing shaping techniques, from short rows and cleverly placed increases and decreases to complex, modular adventures.

And yet, again and again I return to the simplest of shapes: The triangle. My earliest knitting projects were of the top-down, center-out construction that was prevalent at the time, from designers like Nancy Bush, Sharon Miller, Dorothy Siemens, and, of course, Pam Allen—her Little Arrowhead Lace Shawl from an issue of Interweave Knits being one of the very first shawls to come off my needles.

There's just something about the three-sided canvas that facilitates exploration of stitch pattern: How the direction of one's knitting—top down, bottom up, sideways—changes the behavior of the lines within the patterning, whether they converge, or run parallel; how those lines sit within the totality of the canvas and interact with the triangle's three points; how they interact at and with the shawl's center spine (if the construction makes for a defined center line; some do, some don't).

Add to that yarn choice—of which Quince has no shortage of irresistible options—and there's a mountain of possibility to be had with the humble, traditional triangle.

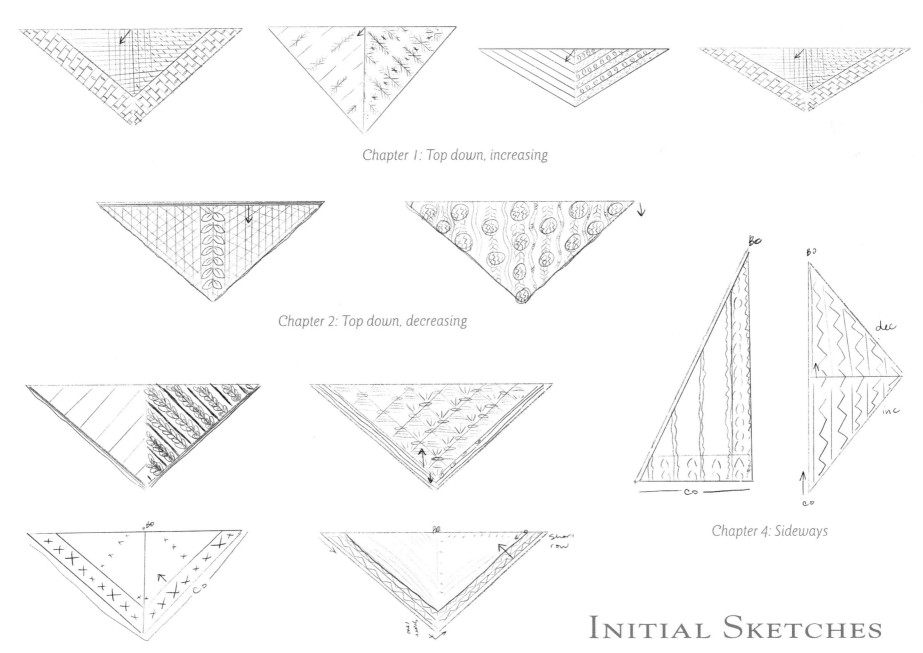

Chapter 1: Top down, increasing

Chapter 2: Top down, decreasing

Chapter 4: Sideways

Chapter 3: Bottom up

INITIAL SKETCHES

9

CHAPTER 1:
Top Down, *Increasing*

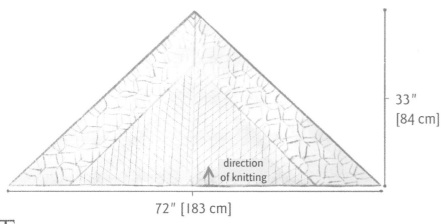

33"
[84 cm]

direction
of knitting

72" [183 cm]

TULSI

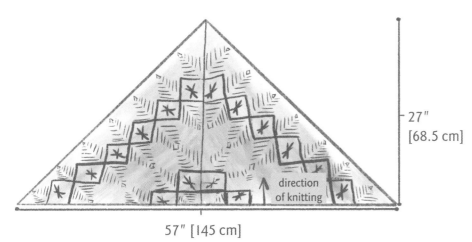

27"
[68.5 cm]

direction
of knitting

57" [145 cm]

BORAGE

TOP DOWN, INCREASING

A method many knitters think of as "traditional" shawl construction, top-down, center-out shawls can be a great starting point for building a knitted triangle.

A simple shape like this usually begins with just a few stitches, oftentimes with a garter tab at the center neck, setting up the starting point for the top edge of the shawl and the foundation of the chosen edge treatment. Shawl increases are set up to occur at each side edge, one pair of increases at the beginning and at the end, and another pair at the center spine, every right side row. The result is an increase rate of 4 stitches every two rows, creating a triangle shape roughly equivalent to half of a square, with a deep central spine.

When developing stitch patterns for this shape, going with even-numbered stitch counts and row repeats that are in multiples divisible by 4 ensures the motifs cleanly resolve within the shaping of this type of three-sided canvas.

TULSI

yarn: chickadee
color: chanterelle

BORAGE

yarn: piper
color: rock springs

Tutorial: Garter Tab

A garter tab is a clever, traditional way to begin a top-down triangular shawl. It features edges kept in garter stitch at the beginning and end of the rows, creating a subtle frame for the main body of the shawl.

Why a tab? Like the name implies, starting a shawl with a garter tab means you create a tiny strip of knitted fabric (a tab, if you will) that is then turned sideways, and stitches are picked up along one side. After picking up the number of stitches instructed, you end by picking up stitches in the cast-on edge. This creates a row that has three sections: The live stitches from the last row worked, the stitches that were picked up along the side, and the stitches picked up from the cast-on edge.

This somewhat three-sided row creates a clean foundation for a top-down triangular shawl, forming an unbroken line of garter stitch at the center of the top edge, between the two shawl halves.

Here, we'll work with a 2-stitch garter tab, but the method is the same no matter how many edge stitches there are. Some patterns will instruct you to cast stitches onto waste yarn; others will simply use the long-tail cast on. The difference is minimal; here, we'll be covering the latter, but try both out and see which one you prefer.

Step 1: Cast on 2 stitches using the long-tail cast on.

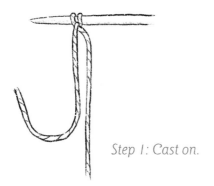

Step 1: Cast on.

Step 2: Knit garter stitch (knit every row) for the number of rows specified in the pattern. This creates a small strip of fabric in garter stitch.

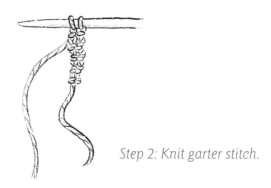

Step 2: Knit garter stitch.

Step 3: (RS) Knit to end of row, but don't turn. Instead, rotate work 90 degrees clockwise, so that the left side of the strip of fabric is now on top, and the two stitches on the right needle are now to the right.

Pick up and knit the required number of stitches instructed in the pattern, evenly spaced along the side edge. This number matches the number of garter ridges that were formed. For example, if the pattern instructs you to pick up 5 stitches, it's likely you worked 10 rows, or 5 garter ridges, plus one last RS row completed. For the cleanest results, pick up into the purl bumps at the edges of the garter ridges (shown above and below in pink).

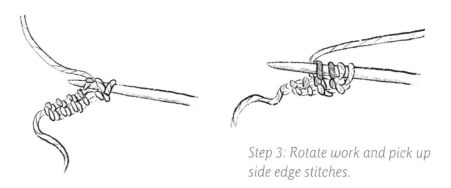

Step 3: Rotate work and pick up side edge stitches.

Step 4: Rotate work again so that cast-on edge is now on top, and picked-up stitches are now on the right. Pick up and knit a stitch in each cast-on stitch, 2 stitches total.

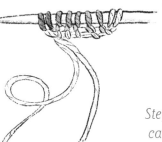

Step 4: Rotate work and pick up cast-on edge stitches.

You now have a completed garter tab, comprised of the live stitches after knitting the strip of garter stitch, the stitches picked up along the side edge (shown in blue), and the stitches picked up along the cast on-edge (shown in green).

The garter tab method creates a smooth, unbroken line along the top edge of a top-down, center-out triangle—the perfect way to begin a shawl like Lemon Balm, shown at right.

Lemon Balm, pages 32-35/106-109

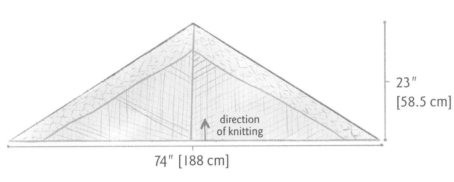

VALERIAN

23"
[58.5 cm]

direction
of knitting

74" [188 cm]

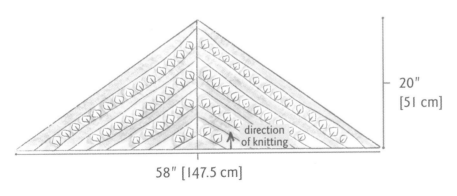

LEMON BALM

20"
[51 cm]

direction
of knitting

58" [147.5 cm]

Top Down, Increasing *(modified)*

A simple but effective modification to the construction covered earlier in this chapter, this method changes the rate of shaping slightly, incorporating an extra pair of edge increases on wrong-side rows. This translates to 6 stitches increased every two rows rather than 4, creating a triangle with a wider wingspan and shallower depth at the central spine (compare the diagrams at left with those on page 13). The extra width of this shape is well suited to wrapping the shawl around the wearer's neck, like a scarf.

Choosing motifs with stitch and row repeats that are a multiple of 6 (12, 18, 24, etc.) allows the patterning to fit neatly within the growing shape of the triangle. Valerian, a modified version of Tulsi, features patterning similar to Tulsi's, with a multiple of 6, rather than 4, which allows it to repeat cleanly within the modified shawl shape.

However, a motif doesn't necessarily have to continue all the way to the shawl's edges, as in the leaf patterns of Lemon Balm, at left. Instead of creating partial repeats that are interrupted by the edge of the triangle, pattern repeats can be designed to begin only when there are enough stitches to work a complete motif. Before that point, working in plain stitches (in this case, reverse stockinette) at the growing shawl edges creates a clean, unbroken pattern.

VALERIAN

yarn: finch
color: shell

Tutorial: Lacy Bind Off

My absolute favorite bind off technique for shawl edges that require some stretch and looseness, the lacy bind off is simple and easy to work. It provides all the elasticity needed to prevent a shawl edge from being bound off too tightly for comfort, as is often the case with a traditional bind off.

The pattern instructions for a lacy bind off state:

K1, *sl 1, insert LH needle into front loops of sts on RH needle and k2tog in this position; rep from * to end.

Let's break it down, step by step.

First, knit 1:

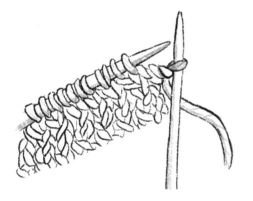

Step 1: Knit 1.

Then, slip the next stitch (as if to purl, unless otherwise stated—you don't want to twist the stitch):

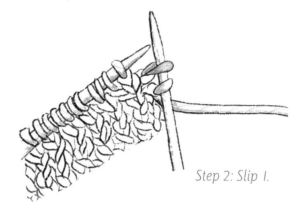

Step 2: Slip 1.

Next, insert the left needle tip into the front loops of the stitches on the right needle (look carefully, and you'll notice that this sets these stitches up to be knitted just like a knit two together through the back loop)...

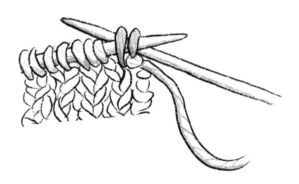

Step 3: Insert left needle tip into front loops.

...and knit them together in that position:

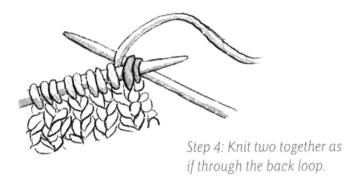

*Step 4: Knit two together as
if through the back loop.*

One stitch has been bound off:

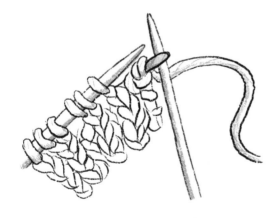

Repeat slipping stitches from left to right needle and knitting the two stitches on the right needle through the back loop, until one stitch remains; break yarn and draw through final loop to fasten off.

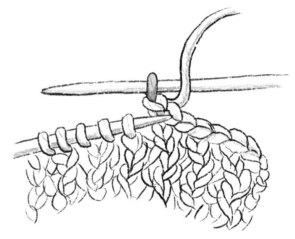

For patterns that instruct you to bind off using the lacy bind off *purlwise*, you'll do the same thing, but in the inverse:

P1, *sl 1, insert LH needle into front loops of sts on RH needle and p2tog in this position; rep from * to end.

LEMON BALM

yarn: tern
color: back bay

CHAPTER 2:
Top Down, *Decreasing*

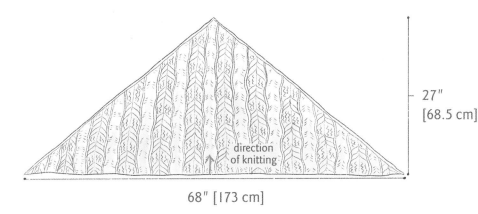

direction
of knitting

27"
[68.5 cm]

68" [173 cm]

CLARY SAGE

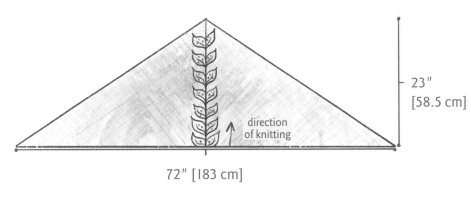

direction
of knitting

23"
[58.5 cm]

72" [183 cm]

NETTLE

TOP DOWN, DECREASING

Unlike the first two top-down constructions covered so far, this method involves casting on the maximum number of stitches that span the top edge of the triangle, then decreasing from there to the bottom point of the shawl, ending with a single stitch to bind off.

Clary Sage and Nettle both feature decreases worked at each side edge every row (both on the right side and the wrong side), with no central spine shaping.

This rate of 4 stitches is similar to the shaping angle created by top down, increasing methods, but with one major difference in the result: With shaping focused to the side edges only, the flow of the motifs retains a vertical line from top edge to bottom point, rather than angled from center spine out to the bottom edges at approximately 45 degrees.

This can create a striking effect of an uninterrupted, allover pattern, as in Clary Sage, or allow for a vertically-oriented central motif, like the ladder of lace leaves in Nettle.

CLARY SAGE

yarn: crane
color: abilene

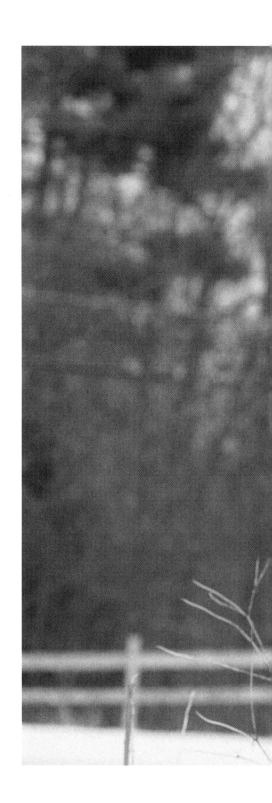

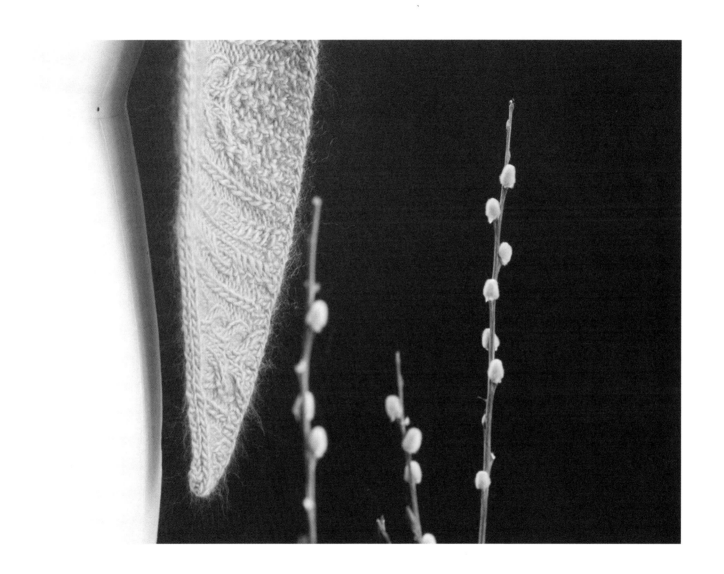

KNIT LITERACY:
UNDERSTANDING CHARTED PATTERNS

A number of the projects in this book use charted patterns and motifs that are too large to provide the written row-by-row instructions that would usually accompany them.

In this section, we cover how to see a knitting chart as a visual depiction of your actual knitting—what to look for, ways to use it to keep your place in your knitting, and, importantly, how read your knitting to anticipate what comes next, with a less frequent need to refer to the chart or written instruction.

First: Read through the pattern, all the way through. Pay particular attention to the special abbreviations and construction notes at the beginning of the pattern, as well as the part of the pattern that instructs you to begin working from a given chart. Often, these sections will provide important details that aren't necessarily displayed on the charts themselves, such as the rate of increase or decrease; whether shawl shaping is included in the chart, or worked in addition to it; and where markers should be placed, if any.

Pay close attention, as well, to the symbol legend and what each of the knitting symbols and abbreviations stand for in the context of the pattern. While modern knitting patterns have come a long way in terms of standardizing the essential abbreviations used, there is no guarantee that the knitting terminology used in the pattern is going to follow the same instruction you're familiar with. A good pattern, however, will provide clear details about every knitting maneuver used.

Chart Basics

All charts are provided with "right side facing"; that is, they are a visual depiction of what the knitting looks like with the public, or right side facing out. Knowing this comes in handy when working a wrong side row—what the chart shows is what that row will look like from the public, right-facing side, so by logic, the opposite action is used (i.e., a knit stitch symbol on a wrong side row is worked as a purl stitch, creating a knit stitch on the right side).

Whether a chart is worked flat or in the round, it is always read from the bottom up, starting with row/round 1—just like the knitting on your needles, which begins at the cast on edge and builds from the bottom up.

Reading a Chart

Once you familiarize yourself with the basics of the shawl's construction, stitch patterns, and the abbreviations and symbols used in the chart, take a visual test drive of the chart itself. A mental checklist could go something like this:

Is the chart worked flat or in the round?

All of the projects in this book are knitted flat, back and forth in rows, so all charts should be read accordingly.

Charts worked flat are typically given with right-side (usually odd-numbered) rows read from right to left—this follows the direction of the actual knitting on your needles, from beginning of the row to the end. Wrong-side (even-numbered) rows are read from left to right, which also follows the direction of knitting on the wrong side, as viewed from the right side—left to right. Since knitting is still worked right to left, no matter which side faces you, the symbol legend will give corresponding actions for working stitches from the wrong side (i.e., a knit stitch symbol is "knit on the RS, purl on the WS").

For charts worked in the round, all rows are worked from right to left—again, think about the direction of knitting: In the round, you are always working with the right side facing, therefore always from right to left.

Arrows at the first two chart rows will also clue you in on how to read the direction of the rows.

What do the pattern instructions say about how to work the chart?

The beauty of knitting charts is the sheer amount of information that can be elegantly displayed in a relatively small space. Usually, a section of the shawl can be condensed into a sliver that represents a much larger area of actual knitting. Because of this efficiency, reading a knitting chart can seem daunting. A good pattern will tell you exactly what to do with the wealth of information packed into a chart.

Take note of the total number of stitches and rows given in the chart:

Chart Rows: Check the pattern instructions to see how many times you're instructed to work full repeats (a repeat being first row to last of the chart), and any partial repeats to finish with before moving on to the next chart or section of the pattern. For example: "Work Rows 1-56 a total of 4 times, then work Rows 1-12 one more time."

Chart Stitches: Charts often have what's referred to as a "bracketed stitch repeat", or more simply put, "pattern repeat". This section of knitting is usually outlined in a special color and labeled as a specific number of stitches to be repeated more than once along a given row. Pattern instructions will tell you how many times to work a repeat when you come to it in a row. For instance, in Clary Sage's Right Pattern chart (see page 113), you're instructed to work the pattern repeat two times. First, knit the stitches that precede the bracket. When you reach the first stitch in the 56-stitch repeat, work all of the stitches within the orange bracket as shown, and then work those same 56 stitches again, before continuing with the remainder of the row.

The pattern instructions will tell you other important things like where to place markers, the number of stitches increased or decreased in a given row, and the total number of stitches on the needles after the row is completed.

How many charts are in the pattern, and how do they fit together?

Getting a sense of how many charts there are and which sections of the pattern they occupy is a good idea, especially taken together with the pattern instructions from start to finish. Some charts simply begin where the previous one left off; in other patterns, there are additional things to do before resuming working with a charted section.

Once you have a fairly comprehensive picture of what the pattern entails, it's time to cast on and begin knitting.

How do I keep track of where I am in the chart?

Easy: Look at your knitting. With time and enough practice, the stitches on your needles and the completed rows flowing out from beneath them are your best indicator of where your next step of the pattern goes. Becoming familiar with the knitting symbols, and how they often visually look like the stitches you are performing, gives you a valuable visual indicator of how different stitches can come together to form elements like cables, lace, or textural knit-purl configurations.

Finding rhythm in a repeat with a mix of stitch patterns is also useful—often, you can find ways to keep track of one element using another, since they tend to occur or repeat at the same rate (or a multiple of it).

Studying the charts before casting on goes a long way towards a smooth and enjoyable project, with only an occasional glance at the pattern to check your work. Which elements coincide? Where do repeats occur?

Let's use a section of the Clary Sage pattern with an overlay of some of its chart symbols as an example, shown on the facing page.

Little details that line up with each other, or relate in some way, can serve as signposts for keeping track without having to follow the chart box by box, stitch by stitch…such as:

a. The first cable crossing row of the larger cable always lines up with the first cable crossing row of the smaller cable.
b. The lace section begins similarly, with the first row lining up with the first crossing rows of both cables.
c. The lace sections have 14 rows (7 lace rows on the RS, 7 plain rows on the WS) and always begin with patterning that starts off with a "k2tog, yo", then alternates in subsequent RS rows with patterning that starts with a "yo, ssk". These lace sections will also always end with a sequence that begins with "k2tog, yo", just like the first lace row.
d. The small cables have 5 RS crossing rows total. Pay attention to where these line up in the other motifs: The fourth crossing lines up with the second crossing in the larger cable.
e. There are 5 rows in plain stockinette (2 knit rows on the RS and 3 purl rows on the WS, beginning with the WS row that follows the cable crossing) in between crossings on the larger cable, which has a total of 3 crossings. After working the WS row following the third crossing, the first row of the lace pattern and the first crossing of the smaller cable line up immediately afterward (which lines up with the larger cable, as referenced in point **a**).
f. The shaping decreases at the beginnings and ends of the rows will always be in rib, with the decrease worked into the second stitch from the ends of the rows, always in the direction leaning towards the center point.
g. Cables near the edges of the piece are only worked if the required amount of stitches exist; where they do not, plain knit stitches are worked instead.

While this doesn't illustrate how to work every last stitch on the chart, these are just a few of the ways to use the major details in patterned knitting to get your bearings, and anticipate what comes next. Refer back to the pattern instructions every once in a while to make sure you're still on the right path!

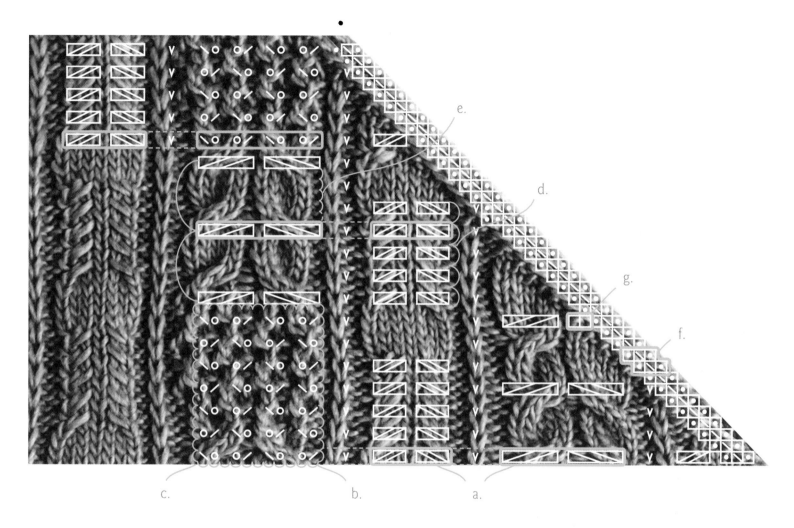

KEEPING TRACK IN CHARTED PATTERNS (CLARY SAGE DETAIL)
See facing page for notes.

NETTLE

yarn: sparrow
color: truffle

Chapter 3:
Bottom Up

Increasing
Decreasing
Sideways Border

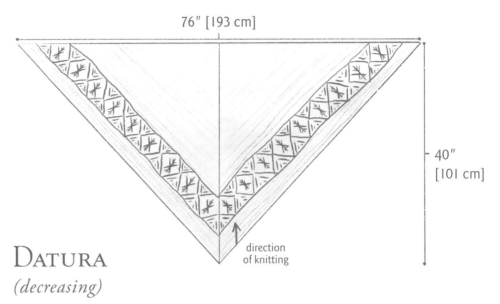

76" [193 cm]

40"
[101 cm]

direction
of knitting

DATURA
(decreasing)

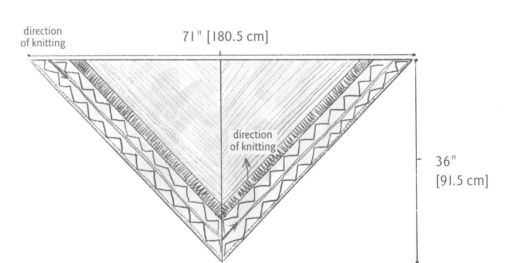

direction
of knitting

71" [180.5 cm]

direction
of knitting

36"
[91.5 cm]

MOONFLOWER
(sideways border)

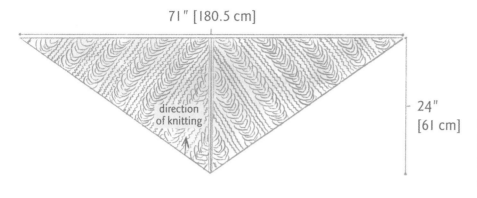

71" [180.5 cm]

direction
of knitting

24"
[61 cm]

MUGWORT
(decreasing)

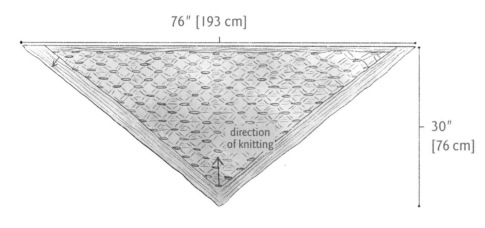

76" [193 cm]

direction
of knitting

30"
[76 cm]

HYSSOP
(increasing)

BOTTOM UP

Similar to top down, decreasing shawls, bottom up construction typically begins by casting on the maximum number of stitches—this time around, for the two bottom edges, rather than the top edge—and working shaping decreases to the center point of the top edge, finishing with a bind off of one or two stitches by the end. Datura features a pretty integrated border as its centerpiece, while Mugwort carries textured cables and rickrack in bold columns towards the shawl's top center.

Decreasing is just one way of working a shawl from the bottom up! In Hyssop, knitting begins at the bottom point and increases from there, until the width of the top edge is achieved. After this main section is completed, stitches are picked up from the bottom edges and worked down, increasing at sides and center point, then bound off.

My favorite method, however, is shown in Moonflower: A sideways knitted border is cast on first, with short rows to shape what will become a side point of the shawl. From there, the border is worked as a strip to the point where short row shaping makes a reappearance, creating the turned corner that forms the bottom tip of the shawl. The border then proceeds to the second half of the border in reverse fashion, and is finished off with short row shaping to form the second side tip.

Once the border is completed, stitches are picked up along the inner edge of the "L" shape of the border, and, similarly to Datura and Mugwort, are shaped by side and central decreases to the center of the top edge.

Bottom up shawls are so satisfying to knit—simple and to the point.

DATURA

yarn: phoebe
color: jupiter

Mugwort

yarn: owl
color: cielo

Moonflower

yarn: owl
color: tyto

Hyssop

yarn: osprey
color: storm

CHAPTER 4:
Sideways

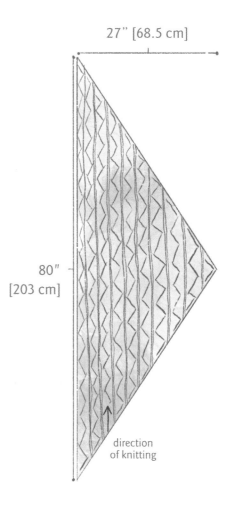

27" [68.5 cm]

80"
[203 cm]

direction
of knitting

REISHI

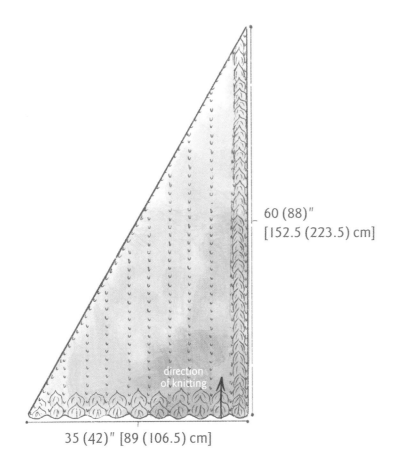

60 (88)"
[152.5 (223.5) cm]

direction
of knitting

35 (42)" [89 (106.5) cm]

CHAGA

SIDEWAYS

The final method of creating a three-sided canvas is the sideways knitted triangle, covered here in two ways:

Chaga begins by casting on for a lacy border along the bottom edge, then by decreasing along the left side only, down to the point at the opposite end. Keeping one edge unshaped allows for a pretty element to be carried up from the border, creating decoratively framed edges for this asymmetrical, right-angled triangle.

In Reishi, you begin by casting on at one side point and increasing along the right edge to the specified width, wherein the shawl's bottom point is formed; from there, increases switch to decreases along the same side, back down to the opposite point. This creates a balanced triangle with stitch patterns that run horizontally, from tip to tip, rather than vertically, or radiating out from a central spine, as with top-down/bottom-up construction.

These constructions open up possibilities for working with motifs that have a strong linear element to them, as is the case with Reishi's zig-zagging lace lines (eagle eyes will recognize this motif from Moonflower's sideways border, used here as an allover pattern).

REISHI
yarn: lark
color: audouin

CHAGA

yarn: crane
color: quanah

Patterns

TULSI

Finished measurements

72" [183 cm] wingspan and 33" [84 cm] deep at center spine

Yarn

Chickadee by Quince & Co
(100% American wool; 181yd [166m]/50g)
- 7 skeins Chanterelle 118

Needles

- One 32" circular needle (circ) in size US 6 [4 mm]
- One 32" circ in size US 7 [4.5 mm]

Or size to obtain gauge

Notions

- Stitch marker
- Cable needle
- Tapestry needle

Gauge

21 sts and 32 rows = 4" [10 cm] in main pattern with smaller needles, after blocking.

Special abbreviations

sl 1: Slip 1 stitch knitwise with yarn held in back.
SCR (smocking cable, leans to the right): Slip 5 stitches onto cable needle (cn) and hold in back, k1, then k1, p2, k2 from cn.
SCL (smocking cable, leans to the left): Slip 1 stitch onto cn and hold in front, k2, p2, k1, then k1 from cn.

Main pattern for swatching (mult of 4 sts)

See also swatching chart, next page.
Row 1: (RS) *K1, p1; rep from * to end.
Row 2: Rep Row 1.
Row 3: *P1, k3; rep from *.
Row 4: *P3, k1; rep from *.
Rows 5 and 6: Rep Rows 1 and 2.
Row 7: (RS) *K2, p1, k1; rep from *.
Row 8: *P1, k1, p2; rep from *.
Repeat Rows 1-8 for main pattern for swatching.

Note

Tulsi is worked flat, from the top down, with increases at each side edge and at center spine every RS row throughout shawl.

SHAWL

With smaller circular needle (circ) and using the long-tail cast on, CO 9 sts. Do not join.

Begin main pattern set up

See also pattern set up chart, this page.

Increases occur every RS row throughout shawl.

Row 1 *place marker:* (RS) K1-f/b, p1, k1, p1, M1R, place marker for center, k1, M1L, p1, k1, p1, k1-f/b (4 sts inc'd)—13 sts.

Row 2: (K1, p1) to 1 st before marker (m), k1, slip marker (sl m), (p1, k1) to end.

Row 3: K1-f/b, k2, p1, k2, M1R, sl m, k1, M1L, k2, p1, k2, k1-f/b—17 sts.

Row 4: K1, *p3, k1; rep from * to end, slipping m.

Begin main pattern

See also main chart, next page.

Row 1: (RS) K1-f/b, p1, (k1, p1) to m, M1R, sl m, k1, M1L, (p1, k1) to last 2 sts, p1, k1-f/b (4 sts inc'd)—21 sts.

Row 2: K1 *p1, k1; rep from * to end, slipping m.

Row 3: K1-f/b, k2, (p1, k3) to 3 sts before m, p1, k2, M1R, sl m, k1, M1L, k2, p1, (k3, p1) to last 3 sts, k2, k1-f/b—25 sts.

Row 4: K1, *p3, k1; rep from * to end, slipping m.

Rep the last 4 rows 42 more times—361 sts.

Work Rows 1 and 2 one more time—365 sts.

Change to larger circ.

Begin border

See also border chart, next page.

Row 1: (RS) K1-f/b, (k2, p2) to 1 st before m, k1, M1R, sl m, k1, M1L, k1, (p2, k2) to last st, k1-f/b (4 sts inc'd)—369 sts.

Row 2: K2, (p2, k2) to 3 sts before m, p2, k1, sl m, p2, (k2, p2) to last 2 sts, k2.

Row 3: K1-f/b, p1, (k2, p2) to 2 sts before m, k2, M1R, sl m, k1, M1L, k2, (p2, k2) to last 2 sts, p1, k1-f/b—373 sts.

Row 4: K3, (p2, k2) to m, sl m, k1, p2, (k2, p2) to last 3 sts, k3.

Row 5: K1-f/b, p2, (k2, p2) to 3 sts before m, k2, p1, M1R, sl m, k1, M1L, p1, k2, (p2, k2) to last 3 sts, p2, k1-f/b—377 sts.

Row 6: K1, p1, k2, (p2, k2) to 5 sts before m, p2, k3, sl m, (k2, p2) to last 4 sts, k2, p1, k1.

Row 7: K1-f/b, k1, p2, k2, p2, (SCR, p2) to 4 sts before m, k2, p2, M1R, sl m, k1, M1L, p2, k2, (p2, SCL) to last 8 sts, p2, k2, p2, k1, k1-f/b—381 sts.

Row 8: K1, (p2, k2) to 2 sts before m, p1, k1, sl m, p1, (k2, p2) to last st, k1.

Rep Rows 1-8 three more times—429 sts.

Work Rows 1-4 one more time—437 sts.

Next row: (RS) Bind off using the lacy bind off as follows: K1, *sl 1, insert LH needle into front loops of sts in RH needle and k2tog in this position; rep from * to end.

Finishing

Weave in ends. Wet block shawl to finished measurements.

KEY

☐	knit on RS, purl on WS
•	purl on RS, knit on WS
2/	k1-f/b
r	M1R
⅂	M1L
⧄	SCR [see Special abbreviations]
⧄	SCL [see Special abbreviations]
☐	pattern repeat
		marker placement
▧	no stitch

SWATCHING PATTERN

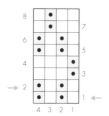

PATTERN SET UP

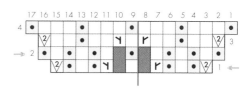

Main pattern

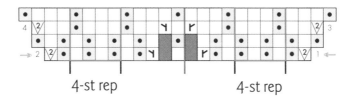

4-st rep   4-st rep

Border pattern

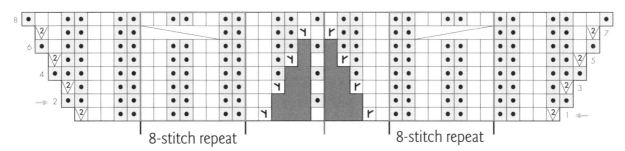

8-stitch repeat   8-stitch repeat

BORAGE

Finished measurements
57" [145 cm] wingspan and 27" [68.5 cm] deep at center

Yarn
Piper by Quince & Co
(50% super kid mohair, 50% South African superfine merino; 305yd [279m]/50g)
- 2 skeins Rock Springs 609

Needles
- One 32" circular needle in size US 7 [4.5 mm]

Or size to obtain gauge

Notions
- Stitch marker
- Cable needle (optional)
- Tapestry needle
- Blocking pins and/or wires (optional)

Gauge
18 sts and 32 rows = 4" [10 cm] in stockinette stitch, after blocking.

Special abbreviations
RPC-tbl: Slip 1 stitch onto cable needle (cn) and hold in back, k1-tbl, then p1 from cn.
LPC-tbl: Slip 1 stitch onto cn and hold in front, p1, then k1-tbl from cn.

Notes
1. Borage is knitted flat, from the top down, beginning from a garter tab, with increases occurring at each side edge and center spine every RS row throughout shawl.
2. Due to the large size of the pattern motif, this pattern is charted only, broken into six charts. Each chart is worked twice to make shawl, repeated on either side of a center spine stitch. One stitch at each side edge and one stitch at center spine do not appear in the charts.
3. In order to make these large charts as small as possible, the stitch pattern repeat may shift from one chart to the next. If you use markers to keep track of repeats, remove them as you go on the final WS row of each chart, then replace them according to the repeat while working Row 1 of the next chart.
4. If you tend to bind off tightly, use a needle one or two sizes larger to bind off.

SHAWL

Using the long-tail cast on, CO 2 sts.

Begin garter tab

First row: (RS) Knit.

Rep this row 10 more times, ending after a RS row. After last row, do not turn work, but pick up and knit 5 sts along the left side of the fabric (1 st in each garter ridge), then pick up and knit 1 st in each CO st—9 sts on needle.

Next row *place marker:* (WS) K2, p2, place marker for center, p3, k2.

Begin stitch pattern

See chart A, next page.

Increases are not charted. Increases occur every RS row throughout shawl.

First row: (RS) K1, M1L, work Row 1 of chart A to 1 st before marker (m), M1R, k1, slip marker (sl m), M1L, work Row 1 of chart A to last st, M1R, k1 (4 sts inc'd)—13 sts.

Next row: K2, work Row 2 of chart A to 1 st before m, p1, sl m, p2, work Row 2 of chart A to last 2 sts, k2.

Work Rows 3-24 of chart A as est—57 sts.

Continue stitch pattern

See chart B, next page.

Next row: (RS) K1, M1L, work Row 25 of chart B to 1 st before m, M1R, k1, sl m, M1L, work Row 25 of chart B to last st, M1R, k1 (4 sts inc'd)—61 sts.

Next row: K2, work Row 26 of chart B to 1 st before m, p1, sl m, p2, work Row 26 of chart B to last 2 sts, k2.

Work Rows 27-56 of chart B as est—121 sts.

Continue stitch pattern

See chart C, page 99.

Next row: (RS) K1, M1L, work Row 57 of chart C to 1 st before m, M1R, k1, sl m, M1L, work Row 57 of chart C to last st, M1R, k1 (4 sts inc'd)—125 sts.

Next row: K2, work Row 58 of chart C to 1 st before m, p1, sl m, p2, work Row 58 of chart C to last 2 sts, k2.

Work Rows 59-80 of chart C as est—169 sts.

Continue stitch pattern

See chart D, page 99.

Next row: (RS) K1, M1L, work Row 81 of chart D to 1 st before m, M1R, k1, sl m, M1L, work Row 81 of chart D to last st, M1R, k1 (4 sts inc'd)—173 sts.

Next row: K2, work Row 82 of chart D to 1 st before m, p1, sl m, p2, work Row 82 of chart D to last 2 sts, k2.

Work Rows 83-104 of chart D as est—217 sts.

Continue stitch pattern

See chart E, page 100.

Next row: (RS) K1, M1L, work Row 105 of chart E to 1 st before m, M1R, k1, sl m, M1L, work Row 105 of chart E to last st, M1R, k1 (4 sts inc'd)—221 sts.

Next row: K2, work Row 106 of chart E to 1 st before m, p1, sl m, p2, work Row 106 of chart E to last 2 sts, k2.

Work Rows 107-136 of chart E as est—281 sts.

Continue stitch pattern

See chart F, page 100.

Next row: (RS) K1, M1L, work Row 137 of chart F to 1 st before m, M1R, k1, sl m, M1L, work Row 137 of chart F to last st, M1R, k1 (4 sts inc'd)—285 sts.

Next row: K2, work Row 138 of chart F to 1 st before m, p1, sl m, p2, work Row 138 of chart F to last 2 sts, k2.

Work Rows 139-163 of chart F as est—337 sts.

Next row: (WS) Bind off loosely knitwise, using a larger needle, if necessary.

Finishing

Weave in ends. Wet block shawl to finished measurements, using blocking pins and/or wires, if you like.

Chart B

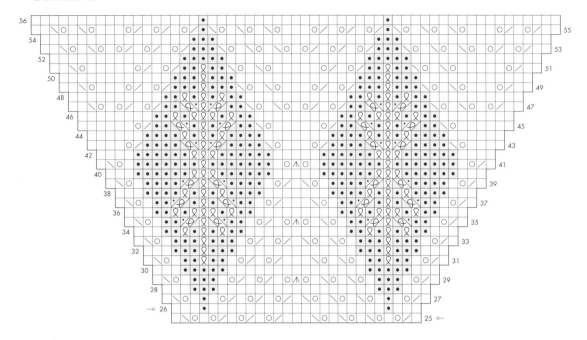

Chart A

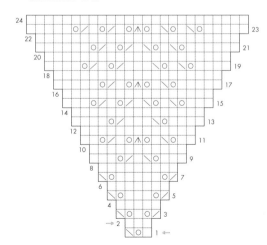

Key

☐	knit on RS, purl on WS
●	purl on RS, knit on WS
◯	yo
╱	k2tog
╲	ssk
⋀	s2kp
℧	k1-tbl on RS, p1-tbl on WS
⟋	RPC-tbl [see Special abbreviations]
⟍	LPC-tbl [see Special abbreviations]
☐	pattern repeat

Chart D

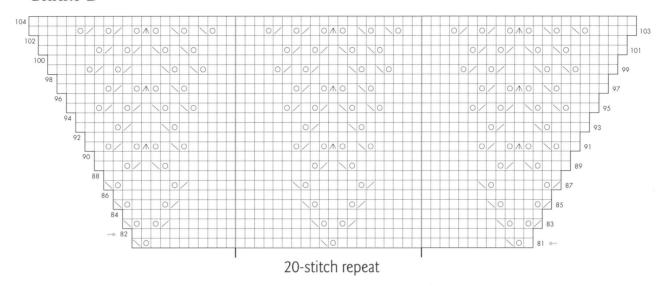

20-stitch repeat

Chart C

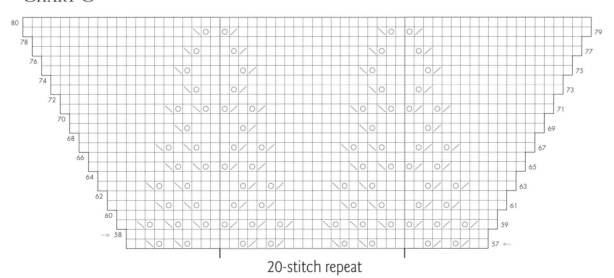

20-stitch repeat

CHART F

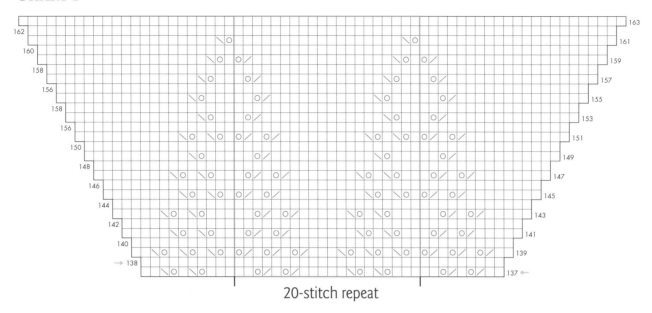

20-stitch repeat

CHART E

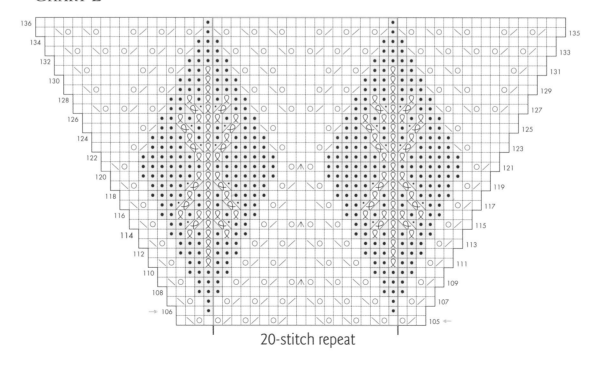

20-stitch repeat

VALERIAN

Finished measurements

74" [188 cm] wingspan and 23" [58.5 cm] deep at center spine

Yarn

Finch by Quince & Co
(100% American wool; 221yd [202m]/50g)

- 6 skeins Shell 171

Needles

- One 32" circular needle (circ) in size US 5 [3.75 mm]
- One 32" circ in size US 6 [4 mm]

Or size to obtain gauge

Notions

- Stitch markers
- Cable needle
- Tapestry needle

Gauge

26 sts and 43 rows = 4" [10 cm] in main pattern with smaller needles, after blocking.

Special abbreviations

sl 1: Slip 1 stitch knitwise with yarn held in back.
SCR (smocking cable, leans to the right): Slip 5 stitches onto cable needle (cn) and hold in back, k1, then k1, p2, k2 from cn.
SCL (smocking cable, leans to the left): Slip 1 stitch onto cn and hold in front, k2, p2, k1, then k1 from cn.

Main pattern for swatching (mult of 6 sts + 1)

Row 1: (RS) *K3, p1, k2; rep from * to last st, k1.
Row 2: P1, *p2, k1, p3; rep from * to end.
Row 3: *K2, (p1, k1) two times; rep from * to last st, k1.
Row 4: P1, *(p1, k1) two times, p2; rep from *.
Row 5: *K1, p1, k3, p1; rep from * to last st, k1.
Row 6: P1, *k1, p3, k1, p1; rep from *.
Row 7: *P1, k2; rep from * to last st, p1.
Row 8: K1, *p2, k1; rep from *.
Rows 9 and 10: Rep Rows 5 and 6.
Rows 11 and 12: Rep Rows 3 and 4.
Repeat Rows 1-12 for main pattern for swatching.

Note

Valerian is knitted flat from the top down, with increases at each side edge every row and at center spine every RS row throughout shawl.

SHAWL

With smaller circular needle (circ) and using the long-tail cast on, CO 7 sts. Do not join.

Begin shawl set up

See also set up chart, next page.

Increases occur every row throughout shawl.

Row 1 *place marker:* (RS) K1-f/b, k1, p1, MIR, place marker for center, k1, MIL, p1, k1, k1-f/b (4 sts inc'd)—11 sts.

Row 2: K1-f/b, p2, k1, p1, k1, slip marker (sl m), p1, k1, p2, k1-f/b (2 sts inc'd)—13 sts.

Row 3: K1-f/b, k2, p1, k1, p1, MIR, sl m, k1, MIL, p1, k1, p1, k2, k1-f/b—17 sts.

Row 4: K1-f/b, p3, k1, (p1, k1) two times, sl m, (p1, k1) two times, p3, k1-f/b—19 sts.

Row 5: K1-f/b, (k1, p1) two times, k3, p1, MIR, sl m, k1, MIL, p1, k3, (p1, k1) two times, k1-f/b—23 sts.

Row 6: K1-f/b, p2, k1, p1, k1, p3, k1, p1, k1, sl m, p1, k1, p3, k1, p1, k1, p2, k1-f/b—25 sts.

Begin main pattern

See also main chart, page 105.

Row 1: (RS) K1-f/b, k4, p1, (k5, p1) to marker (m), MIR, sl m, k1, MIL, (p1, k5) to last 6 sts, p1, k4, k1-f/b (4 sts inc'd)—29 sts.

Row 2: K1-f/b, (p5, k1) to 2 sts before m, p1, k1, sl m, p1, (k1, p5) to last st, k1-f/b (2 sts inc'd)—31 sts.

Row 3: K1-f/b, k1, (p1, k3, p1, k1) to 1 st before m, p1, MIR, sl m, k1, MIL, p1, (k1, p1, k3, p1) to last 2 sts, k1, k1-f/b—35 sts.

Row 4: K1-f/b, k1, p1, (k1, p3, k1, p1) to 3 sts before m, k1, p1, k1, sl m, p1, k1, (p1, k1, p3, k1) to last 3 sts, p1, k1, k1-f/b—37 sts.

Row 5: K1-f/b, p1, k2, (k1, p1, k1, p1, k2) to 2 sts before m, k1, p1, MIR, sl m, k1, MIL, p1, k1, (k2, p1, k1, p1, k1) to last 4 sts, k2, p1, k1-f/b—41 sts.

Row 6: K1-f/b, p1, k1, p2, (p1, k1, p1, k1, p2) to 4 sts before m, (p1, k1) two times, sl m, p1, k1, p1, (p2, k1, p1, k1, p1) to last 5 sts, p2, k1, p1, k1-f/b—43 sts.

Row 7: K1-f/b, k1, p1, (k2, p1) to m, MIR, sl m, k1, MIL, (p1, k2) to last 3 sts, p1, k1, k1-f/b—47 sts.

Row 8: K1-f/b, (p2, k1) to 2 sts before m, p1, k1, sl m, p1, (k1, p2) to last st, k1-f/b—49 sts.

Row 9: K1-f/b, k1, (k1, p1, k1, p1, k2) to 4 sts before m, (k1, p1) two times, MIR, sl m, k1, MIL, (p1, k1) two times, (k2, p1, k1, p1, k1) to last 2 sts, k1, k1-f/b—53 sts.

Row 10: K1-f/b, p2, (p1, k1, p1, k1, p2) to 6 sts before m, (p1, k1) three times, sl m, p1, (k1, p1) two times, (p2, k1, p1, k1, p1) to last 3 sts, p2, k1-f/b—55 sts.

Row 11: K1-f/b, k1, p1, k1, (p1, k3, p1, k1) to 5 sts before m, p1, k3, p1, MIR, sl m, k1, MIL, p1, k3, p1, (k1, p1, k3, p1) to last 4 sts, k1, p1, k1, k1-f/b—59 sts.

Row 12: K1-f/b, p2, k1, p1, (k1, p3, k1, p1) to 1 st before m, k1, sl m, (p1, k1, p3, k1) to last 5 sts, p1, k1, p2, k1-f/b—61 sts.

Rep the last 12 rows 11 more times—457 sts on needle.

Change to larger circ.

Begin border

See also border chart A, page 105.

Row 1: (RS) K1-f/b, p1, (k1, p1) to m, MIR, sl m, k1, MIL, (p1, k1) to last 2 sts, p1, k1-f/b (4 sts inc'd)—461 sts.

Row 2: K1-f/b, (p1, k1) to m, sl m, p1, (k1, p1) to last st, k1-f/b (2 sts inc'd)—463 sts.

Row 3: K1-f/b, k1, p2, (k2, p2) to 3 sts before m, k2, p1, MIR, sl m, k1, MIL, p1, k2, (p2, k2) to last 4 sts, p2, k1, k1-f/b—467 sts.

Row 4: K1-f/b, (p2, k2) to 5 sts before m, p2, k3, sl m, (k2, p2) to last st, k1-f/b—469 sts.

Row 5: K1-f/b, p1, (k2, p2) to m, MIR, sl m, k1, MIL, (p2, k2) to last 2 sts, p1, k1-f/b—473 sts.

Row 6: K1-f/b, k2, (p2, k2) to 2 sts before m, p1, k1, sl m, p1, (k2, p2) to last 3 sts, k2, k1-f/b—475 sts.

Row 7: K1-f/b, k1, p2, k2, (SCR, p2) to 5 sts before m, k2, p2, k1, MIR, sl m, k1, MIL, k1, p2, k2, (p2, SCL) to last 8 sts, p2, k2, p2, k1, k1-f/b—479 sts.

Row 8: K1-f/b, (p2, k2) to 3 sts before m, p2, k1, sl m, p2, (k2, p2) to last st, k1-f/b—481 sts.

Row 9: K1-f/b, p1, (k2, p2) to 2 sts before m, k2, MIR, sl m, k1, MIL, k2, (p2, k2) to last 2 sts, p1, k1-f/b—485 sts.

Row 10: K1-f/b, k2, (p2, k2) to m, sl m, k1, p2, (k2, p2) to last 3 sts, k2, k1-f/b—487 sts.

Row 11: K1-f/b, k1, p2, (k2, p2) to 3 sts before m, k2, p1, MIR, sl m, k1, MIL, p1, k2, (p2, k2) to last 4 sts, p2, k1, k1-f/b—491 sts.

Row 12: K1-f/b, (p2, k2) to 5 sts before m, p2, k3, sl m, (k2, p2) to last st, k1-f/b—493 sts.

Row 13: K1-f/b, p1, SCR, (p2, SCR) to 6 sts before m, p2, k2, p2, MIR, sl m, k1, MIL, p2, k2, p2, (SCL, p2) to last 8 sts, SCL, p1, k1-f/b—497 sts.

Row 14: K1-f/b, (k2, p2) to 4 sts before m, k2, p1, k1, sl m, p1, k2, (p2, k2) to last st, k1-f/b—499 sts.

Row 15: K1-f/b, k1, (p2, k2) to 3 sts before m, p2, k1, MIR, sl m, k1, MIL, k1, p2, (k2, p2) to last 2 sts, k1, k1-f/b—503 sts.

Row 16: K1-f/b, p2, (k2, p2) to 1 st before m, k1, sl m, (p2, k2) to last 3 sts, p2, k1-f/b—505 sts.

Row 17: K1-f/b, p1, k2, (p2, k2) to m, MIR, sl m, k1, MIL, (k2, p2) to last 4 sts, k2, p1, k1-f/b—509 sts.

Row 18: K1-f/b, (k2, p2) to 2 sts before m, k2, sl m, k1, (p2, k2) to last st, k1-f/b—511 sts.

Row 19: K1-f/b, k1, p2, (SCR, p2) to 3 sts before m, k2, p1, MIR, sl m, k1, MIL, p1, k2, (p2, SCL) to last 4 sts, p2, k1, k1-f/b—515 sts.

Row 20: K1-f/b, (p2, k2) to 5 sts before m, p2, k3, sl m, (k2, p2) to last st, k1-f/b—517 sts.

Continue border pattern

See also border chart B, page 105.

Row 21: (RS) K1-f/b, p1, (k2, p2) to m, MIR, sl m, k1, MIL, (p2, k2) to last 2 sts, p1, k1-f/b (4 sts inc'd)—521 sts.

Row 22: K1-f/b, k2, (p2, k2) to 2 sts before m, p1, k1, sl m, p1, (k2, p2) to last 3 sts, k2, k1-f/b (2 sts inc'd)—523 sts.

Row 23: K1-f/b, k1, p2, (k2, p2) to 1 st before m, k1, MIR, sl m, k1, MIL, k1, (p2, k2) to last 4 sts, p2, k1, k1-f/b—527 sts.

Row 24: K1-f/b, (p2, k2) to 3 sts before m, p2, k1, sl m, p2, (k2, p2) to last st, k1-f/b—529 sts.

Row 25: K1-f/b, p1, k2, p2, (SCR, p2) to 2 sts before m, k2, MIR, sl m, k1, MIL, k2, (p2, SCL) to last 6 sts, p2, k2, p1, k1-f/b—533 sts.

Row 26: K1-f/b, k2, (p2, k2) to m, sl m, k1, p2, (k2, p2) to last 3 sts, k2, k1-f/b—535 sts.

Row 27: K1-f/b, k1, p2, (k2, p2) to 3 sts before m, k2, p1, MIR, sl m, k1, MIL, p1, k2, (p2, k2) to last 4 sts, p2, k1, k1-f/b—539 sts.

Row 28: K1-f/b, (p2, k2) to 5 sts before m, p2, k3, sl m, (k2, p2) to last st, k1-f/b—541 sts.

Row 29: K1-f/b, p1, (k2, p2) to m, MIR, sl m, k1, MIL, (p2, k2) to last 2 sts, p1, k1-f/b—545 sts.

Row 30: K1-f/b, k2, (p2, k2) to 2 sts before m, p1, k1, sl m, p1, (k2, p2) to last 3 sts, k2, k1-f/b—547 sts.

Row 31: K1-f/b, k1, p2, k2, (p2, SCR) to 3 sts before m, p2, k1, MIR, sl m, k1, MIL, k1, p2, (SCR, p2) to last 6 sts, k2, p2, k1, k1-f/b—551 sts.

Row 32: K1-f/b, p2, (k2, p2) to 1 st before m, k1, sl m, (p2, k2) to last 3 sts, p2, k1-f/b—553 sts.

Row 33: K1-f/b, p1, k2, (p2, k2) to m, MIR, sl m, k1, MIL, (k2, p2) to last 4 sts, k2, p1, k1-f/b—557 sts.

Row 34: K1-f/b, (k2, p2) to 2 sts before m, k2, sl m, k1, (p2, k2) to last st, k1-f/b—559 sts.

Row 35: K1-f/b, k1, (p2, k2) to 1 st before m, p1, MIR, sl m, k1, MIL, p1, (k2, p2) to last 2 sts, k1, k1-f/b—563 sts.

Row 36: K1-f/b, p2, (k2, p2) to 3 sts before m, k3, sl m, k2, (p2, k2) to last 3 sts, p2, k1-f/b—565 sts.

Row 37: K1-f/b, p1, (SCR, p2) to m, MIR, sl m, k1, MIL, (p2, SCL) to last 2 sts, p1, k1-f/b—569 sts.

Row 38: K1-f/b, k2, (p2, k2) to 2 sts before m, p1, k1, sl m, p1, (k2, p2) to last 3 sts, k2, k1-f/b—571 sts.

Row 39: K1-f/b, k1, p2, (k2, p2) to 1 st before m, k1, MIR, sl m, k1, MIL, k1, (p2, k2) to last 4 sts, p2, k1, k1-f/b—575 sts.

Row 40: K1-f/b, (p2, k2) to 3 sts before m, p2, k1, sl m, p2, (k2, p2) to last st, k1-f/b—579 sts.

Row 41: K1-f/b, p1, (k1, p1) to m, MIR, sl m, k1, MIL, (p1, k1) to last 2 sts, p1, k1-f/b—583 sts.

Row 42: K1-f/b, p1, *k1, p1; rep from * to last st, k1-f/b—585 sts.

Next row: (RS) Bind off using the lacy bind off as follows: K1, *sl 1, insert LH needle into front loops of sts on RH needle and k2tog in this position; rep from * to end.

Finishing

Weave in ends. Wet block shawl to finished measurements.

KEY

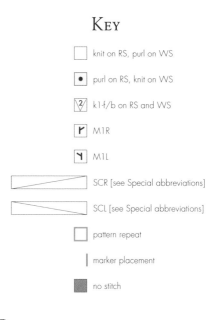

☐	knit on RS, purl on WS
•	purl on RS, knit on WS
2	k1-f/b on RS and WS
r	MIR
⅃	MIL
⟍	SCR [see Special abbreviations]
⟋	SCL [see Special abbreviations]
☐	pattern repeat
		marker placement
■	no stitch

SET UP

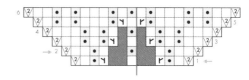

Main pattern

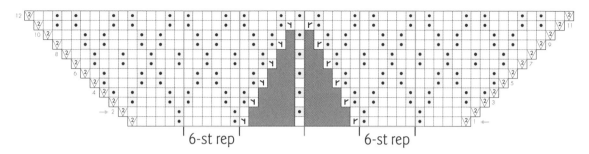

6-st rep   6-st rep

Border A

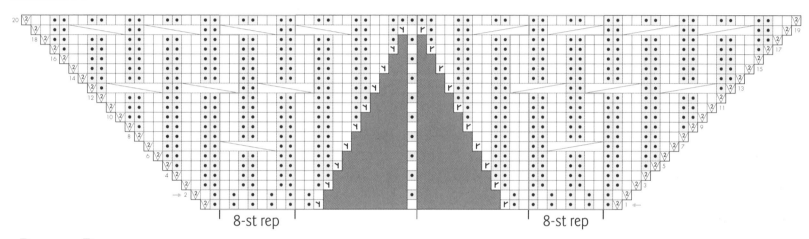

8-st rep   8-st rep

Border B

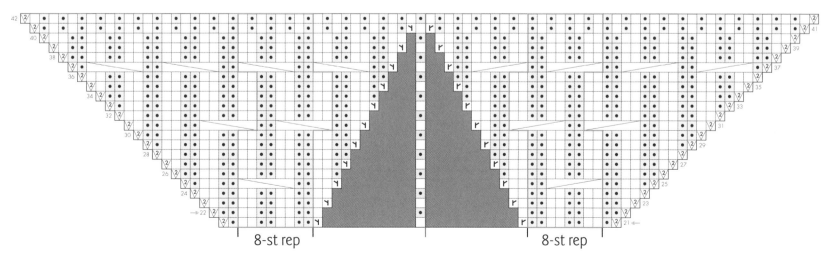

8-st rep   8-st rep

LEMON BALM

Finished measurements

58" [147.5 cm] wingspan and 20" [51 cm] deep at center

Yarn

Tern by Quince & Co
(75% American wool, 25% silk; 221yd [202m]/50g)

• 4 skeins Back Bay 411

Needles

• One 32" circular needle in size US 5 [3.75 mm]

Or size to obtain gauge

Notions

• Stitch markers
• Tapestry needle

Gauge

24 sts and 36 rows = 4" [10 cm] in eyelet pattern, after blocking

24 sts and 40 rows = 4" [10 cm] in leaf pattern, after blocking.

Special abbreviations

yo2: Bring yarn over needle twice. Unless otherwise specified, on the next row, purl into the first yarn over, then purl the second yarn over through the back loop (1 stitch increased).

Eyelet pattern for swatching (mult of 4 sts + 2)

See also eyelet swatching chart, page 109.

Row 1: (RS) K1, yo, ssk, *k2tog, yo2, ssk; rep from * to last 3 sts, k2tog, yo, k1.

Row 2: *Purl to yo2, (p1, p1-tbl) into yo2; rep from * for each yo2, purl to end.

Row 3: K1, *k2tog, yo2, ssk; rep from * to last st, k1.

Row 4: Rep Row 2.

Repeat Rows 1-4 for eyelet pattern for swatching.

Leaf pattern (mult of 12 sts + 11)

See also leaf chart, page 109.

Row 1: (RS) *P5, k1, p6; rep from * to last 11 sts, p5, k1, p5.

Row 2: K5, p1, k5, *k6, p1, k5; rep from * to end.

Row 3: *P4, k3, p5; rep from * to last 11 sts, p4, k3, p4.

Row 4: K4, p3, k4, *k5, p3, k4; rep from *.

Row 5: *P3, k2tog, yo, k1, yo, ssk, p4; rep from * to last 11 sts, p3, k2tog, yo, k1, yo, ssk, p3.

Row 6: K3, p5, k3, *k4, p5, k3; rep from *.

Row 7: *P2, k2tog, (k1, yo) two times, k1, ssk, p3; rep from * to last 11 sts, p2, k2tog, (k1, yo) two times, k1, ssk, p2.

Row 8: K2, p7, k2, *k3, p7, k2; rep from *.

Row 9: *P1, k2tog, k2, yo, k1, yo, k2, ssk, p2; rep from * to last 11 sts, p1, k2tog, k2, yo, k1, yo, k2, ssk, p1.

Row 10: K1, p9, k1, *k2, p9, k1; rep from *.

Row 11: *P1, yo, ssk, k5, k2tog, yo, p2; rep from * to last 11 sts, p1, yo, ssk, k5, k2tog, yo, p1.

Row 12: K1, k1-tbl, p7, k1-tbl, k1, *k2, k1-tbl, p7, k1-tbl, k1; rep from *.

Row 13: *P2, yo, ssk, k3, k2tog, yo, p3; rep from * to last 11 sts, p2, yo, ssk, k3, k2tog, yo, p2.

Row 14: K2, k1-tbl, p5, k1-tbl, k2, *k3, k1-tbl, p5, k1-tbl, k2; rep from *.

Row 15: *P3, yo, ssk, k1, k2tog, yo, p4; rep from * to last 11 sts, p3, yo, ssk, k1, k2tog, yo, p3.

Row 16: K3, k1-tbl, p3, k1-tbl, k3, *k4, k1-tbl, p3, k1-tbl, k3; rep from *.

Row 17: *P4, yo, s2kp, yo, p5; rep from * to last 11 sts, p4, yo, s2kp, yo, p4.

Row 18: K4, k1-tbl, p1, k1-tbl, k4, *k5, k1-tbl, p1, k1-tbl, k4; rep from *.

Row 19: Purl.

Row 20: Knit.

Note

Lemon Balm is worked flat, from the top down, beginning from a garter tab and worked in alternating bands of eyelet and leaf patterns. Stitches are increased at each side edge every row and at center spine every RS row throughout shawl.

SHAWL

Using the long-tail cast on, CO 2 sts.

Begin garter tab

First row: (RS) Knit.

Rep this row 10 more times, ending after a RS row. After last row, do not turn work, but pick up and knit 5 sts along the left side of the fabric (1 st in each garter ridge), then pick up and knit 1 st in each CO st—9 sts on needle.

Next row *place marker:* (WS) K2, p3, place marker for center (pm), p2, k2.

Begin shawl increases

Next row: (RS) K1, k1-f/b, k2, M1R, slip marker (sl m), k1, M1L, k2, k1-f/b, k1 (4 sts inc'd)—13 sts.

Next row: K1, k1-f/b, purl to 1 st before marker (m), k1, sl m, purl to last 2 sts, k1-f/b, k1 (2 sts inc'd)—15 sts.

Begin eyelet pattern

See also eyelet chart, page 109.

Increases occur every row throughout shawl.

On WS rows, (p1, p1-tbl) into each yo2.

Row 1: (RS) K1, k1-f/b, (k2tog, yo2, ssk) to 1 st before m, k1, M1R, sl m, k1, M1L, k1, (k2tog, yo2, ssk) to last 2 sts, k1-f/b, k1 (4 sts inc'd)—19 sts.

Row 2 and all WS rows: K1, k1-f/b, purl to 1 st before m, k1, sl m, purl to last 2 sts, k1-f/b, k1 (2 sts inc'd)—21 sts.

Row 3: K1, k1-f/b, (k2tog, yo2, ssk) to m, M1R, sl m, k1, M1L, (k2tog, yo2, ssk) to last 2 sts, k1-f/b, k1—25 sts.

Row 5: K1, k1-f/b, (k2tog, yo2, ssk) to 3 sts before m, k2tog, yo, k1, M1R, sl m, k1, M1L, k1, yo, ssk, (k2tog, yo2, ssk) to last 2 sts, k1-f/b, k1—31 sts.

Row 7: K1, k1-f/b, (k2tog, yo2, ssk) to 2 sts before m, k2tog, yo, M1R, sl m, k1, M1L, yo, ssk, (k2tog, yo2, ssk) to last 2 sts, k1-f/b, k1—37 sts.

Rows 9-12: Rep Rows 1-4—51 sts.

Begin leaf pattern

Next row *place markers:* (RS) K1, k1-f/b, pm for pattern, work Row 1 of leaf pattern to m, pm for pattern, m1-p/R, sl m, k1, m1-p/L, pm for pattern, work Row 1 of leaf pattern to last 2 sts, pm for pattern, k1-f/b, k1 (4 sts inc'd)—55 sts.

Next row: K1, k1-f/b, knit to pattern m, work Row 2 of patt to next pattern m, sl m, knit to center m, sl m, knit to next pattern m, work Row 2 of patt to next pattern m, sl m, knit to last 2 sts, k1-f/b, k1 (2 sts inc'd)—57 sts.

Next row: K1, k1-f/b, purl to pattern m, work next row of patt to next pattern m, sl m, purl to center m, m1-p/R, sl m, k1, m1-p/L, purl to next pattern m, work next row of patt to next pattern m, sl m, purl to last 2 sts, k1-f/b, k1—61 sts.

Next row: K1, k1-f/b, knit to pattern m, work next row of patt to next pattern m, sl m, knit to center m, sl m, knit to next pattern m, work next row of patt to next pattern m, sl m, knit to last 2 sts, k1-f/b, k1 (2 sts inc'd)—63 sts.

Rep the last 2 rows until all rows of leaf patt have been worked, removing pattern markers on final row—111 sts.

Continue eyelet pattern

Next row: (RS) Work Row 1 of eyelet patt to end (4 sts inc'd)—115 sts.

Cont as est until Rows 1-12 of eyelet patt have been worked—147 sts.

Continue leaf pattern

Next row *place markers:* (RS) K1, k1-f/b, pm for pattern, work Row 1 of leaf pattern to center m, pm for pattern, m1-p/R, sl m, k1, m1-p/L, pm for pattern, work Row 1 of leaf pattern to last 2 sts, pm for pattern, k1-f/b, k1 (4 sts inc'd)—151 sts.

Next row: K1, k1-f/b, knit to pattern m, work Row 2 of patt to next pattern m, sl m, knit to center m, sl m, knit to next pattern m, work Row 2 of patt to next pattern m, sl m, knit to last 2 sts, k1-f/b, k1 (2 sts inc'd)—153 sts.

Next row: K1, k1-f/b, purl to pattern m, work next row of patt to next pattern m, sl m, purl to center m, m1-p/R, sl m, k1, m1-p/L, purl to next pattern m, work next row of patt to next pattern m, sl m, purl to last 2 sts, k1-f/b, k1—157 sts.

Next row: K1, k1-f/b, knit to pattern m, work next row of patt to next pattern m, sl m, knit to center m, sl m, knit to next pattern m, work next row of patt to next pattern m, sl m, knit to last 2 sts, k1-f/b, k1 (2 sts inc'd)—159 sts.

Rep the last 2 rows until all rows of leaf patt have been worked, removing pattern markers on final row—207 sts.

Continue eyelet pattern

Next row: (RS) Work Row 1 of eyelet patt to end (4 sts inc'd)—211 sts.

Cont as est until Rows 1-12 of eyelet patt have been worked—243 sts.

Continue leaf pattern

Next row *place markers:* (RS) K1, k1-f/b, pm for pattern, work Row 1 of leaf pattern to center m, pm for pattern, m1-p/R, sl m, k1, m1-p/L, pm for pattern, work Row 1 of leaf pattern to last 2 sts, pm for pattern, k1-f/b, k1 (4 sts inc'd)—247 sts.

Next row: K1, k1-f/b, knit to pattern m, work Row 2 of patt to next pattern m, sl m, knit to center m, sl m, knit to next pattern m, work Row 2 of patt to next pattern m, sl m, knit to last 2 sts, k1-f/b, k1 (2 sts inc'd)—249 sts.

Next row: K1, k1-f/b, purl to pattern m, work next row of patt to next pattern m, sl m, purl to center m, m1-p/R, sl m, k1, m1-p/L, purl to next pattern m, work next row of patt to next pattern m, sl m, purl to last 2 sts, k1-f/b, k1—253 sts.

Next row: K1, k1-f/b, knit to pattern m, work next row of patt to next pattern m, sl m, knit to center m, sl m, knit to next pattern m, work next row of patt to next pattern m, sl m, knit to last 2 sts, k1-f/b, k1 (2 sts inc'd)—255 sts.

Rep the last 2 rows until all rows of leaf patt have been worked, removing pattern markers on final row—303 sts.

Continue eyelet pattern

Next row: (RS) Work Row 1 of eyelet patt to end (4 sts inc'd)—307 sts.

Cont as est until Rows 1-12 of eyelet patt have been worked—339 sts.

Continue leaf pattern

Next row *place markers:* (RS) K1, k1-f/b, pm for pattern, work Row 1 of leaf pattern to center m, pm for pattern, m1-p/R, sl m, k1, m1-p/L, pm for pattern, work Row 1 of leaf pattern to last 2 sts, pm for pattern, k1-f/b, k1 (4 sts inc'd)—343 sts.

Next row: K1, k1-f/b, knit to pattern m, work Row 2 of patt to next pattern m, sl m, knit to center m, sl m, knit to next pattern m, work Row 2 of patt to next pattern m, sl m, knit to last 2 sts, k1-f/b, k1 (2 sts inc'd)—345 sts.

Next row: K1, k1-f/b, purl to pattern m, work next row of patt to next pattern m, sl m, purl to center m, m1-p/R, sl m, k1, m1-p/L, purl to next pattern m, work next row of patt to next pattern m, sl m, purl to last 2 sts, k1-f/b, k1—349 sts.

Next row: K1, k1-f/b, knit to pattern m, work next row of patt to next pattern m, sl m, knit to center m, sl m, knit to next pattern m, work next row of patt to next pattern m, sl m, knit to last 2 sts, k1-f/b, k1 (2 sts inc'd)—351 sts.

Rep the last 2 rows until all rows of leaf patt have been worked, removing pattern markers on final row—399 sts.

Continue eyelet pattern

Next row: (RS) Work Row 1 of eyelet patt to end (4 sts inc'd)—403 sts.

Cont as est until Rows 1-11 of eyelet patt have been worked—433 sts.

Next row: (WS) K2, [p2, (k1, p1) in yo2] to 3 sts before center m, p2, k1, sl m, [p2, (k1, p1) in yo2] to last 4 sts, p2, k2.

Begin rib trim

Next row: (RS) (K2, p2) to 1 st before m, k1, sl m, (p2, k2) to end.

Next row: (P2, k2) to center m, sl m, k1, (k2, p2) to end.

Next row: (RS) Bind off using the lacy bind off as follows: P2, return 2 sts to LH needle, *p2tog-tbl, return st to LH needle; rep from * to end.

Finishing

Weave in ends. Wet block shawl to finished measurements.

Leaf pattern

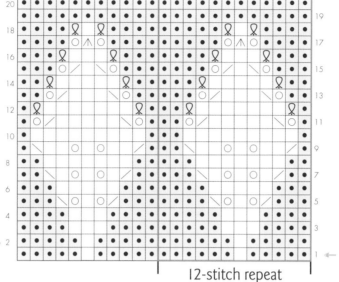

12-stitch repeat

Eyelet swatching pattern

4-st rep

Key

☐	knit on RS, purl on WS
●	purl on RS, knit on WS
☑2	k1-f/b on RS and WS
○	yo
○ ○	yo2
╱	k2tog
╲	ssk
Ͱ	M1L
⊦	M1R
☒	p1-tbl on WS
☒	k1-tbl on WS
⋀	s2kp
▨	no stitch
☐	pattern repeat
		marker placement

Eyelet pattern

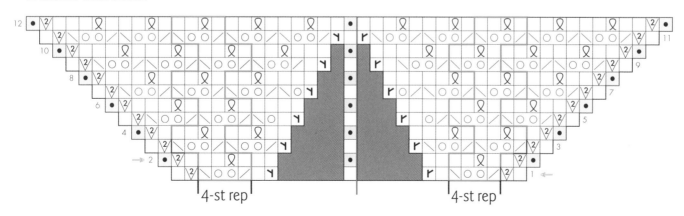

4-st rep   4-st rep

CLARY SAGE

Finished measurements
68" [173 cm] wingspan and 27" [68.5 cm] deep at center spine

Yarn
Crane by Quince & Co
(50% super kid mohair, 50% superfine merino; 208yd [146m]/~100g)
- 4 skeins Abilene 602

Needles
- One 32" circular needle in size US 8 [5 mm]

Or size to obtain gauge

Notions
- Stitch markers
- Cable needle (optional)
- Tapestry needle

Gauge
20 sts and 26 rows = 4" [10 cm] in cable and lace pattern, after blocking.

Special abbreviations
sl 1: Slip 1 stitch purlwise with yarn in back.
C1R (cross 1 over 2 right): Slip 2 stitches onto cable needle (cn) and hold in back, k1, then k2 from cn.
C1L (cross 1 over 2 left): Slip 1 stitch onto cn and hold in front, k2, then k1 from cn.
C2R (cross 2 over 3 right): Slip 3 stitches onto cn and hold in back, k2, then k3 from cn.
C2L (cross 2 over 3 left): Slip 2 stitches onto cn and hold in front, k3, then k2 from cn.

Notes
1. Clary Sage is knitted flat from the top down, beginning at wide top edge and decreased to bottom point. Decreases occur at each side edge every row throughout shawl.
2. Due to the large size of the pattern motif, this pattern is charted only. The main decrease section is divided into two charts and spans two pages, broken at the center marker. The end chart remains in one piece, and is located on the following page.

SHAWL

Using the long-tail cast on, CO 353 sts.

Begin rib trim and shawl decreases

Decreases occur every row throughout shawl.

First row: (WS) P1, k1, p2tog, *k1, p1; rep from * to last 5 sts, k1, ssp, k1, p1 (2 sts dec'd)—351 sts rem.

Next row: K1, p1, ssk, p2, *k1, p1; rep from * to last 5 sts, p1, k2tog, p1, k1 (2 sts dec'd)—349 sts rem.

Next row *place markers:* P1, k1, p2tog, k1, (p1, k1) 29 times, place marker for pattern repeat (pm), (p1, k1) 28 times, pm for patt rep, (p1, k1) 28 times, pm for center, (p1, k1) 28 times, pm for patt rep, (p1, k1) 28 times, pm for patt rep, (p1, k1) 29 times, ssp, k1, p1—347 sts rem.

When viewing the RS, there are 61 sts to first marker, 56 sts between each set of markers, and 62 sts from last marker to end.

Begin stitch pattern

See right and left charts, next two pages.
Slip markers as you come to them.

Next row: (RS) Work Row 1 of right chart to first patt marker (m), work pattern repeat for Row 1 of right chart two times to center m, work patt rep for Row 1 of left chart two times to last m, cont Row 1 of left chart to end (2 sts dec'd)—345 sts rem.

Next row: Work left chart to first patt m, work patt rep for left chart two times to center m, work patt rep for right chart two times to last m, cont right chart to end (2 sts dec'd)—343 sts rem.

Work Rows 3-55 of charts as est—237 sts rem.

Row 56 *remove markers:* (WS) Work left chart to first patt m, remove m, work patt rep for left chart two times to center m, work patt rep for right chart two times to last m, remove m, cont right chart to end—235 sts rem.

Continue stitch pattern

Next row: (RS) Work Row 1 of right chart to center m, work Row 1 of left chart to end (2 sts dec'd)—233 sts rem.

Next row: Work left chart to center m, work right chart to end (2 sts dec'd)—231 sts rem.

Work Rows 3-56 as est, removing all markers on final row—123 sts rem.

End stitch pattern

See end chart, page 114.

Next row: (RS) Work Row 1 of end chart (2 sts dec'd)—121 sts rem.

Next row: Work Row 2 of end chart (2 sts dec'd)—119 sts rem.

Work Rows 3-61 of chart—1 st rem.

Cut yarn and draw through rem st.

Finishing

Weave in ends. Wet block shawl to finished measurements.

Key

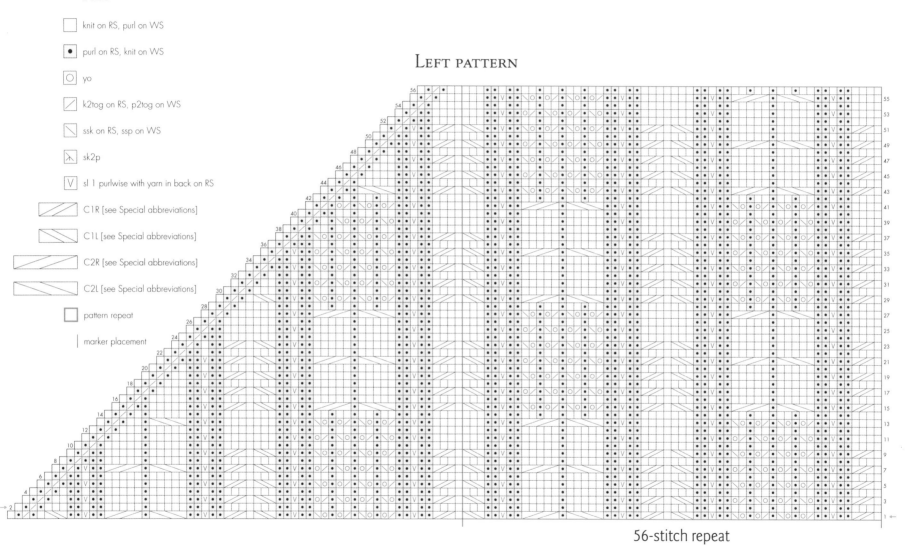

☐ knit on RS, purl on WS

• purl on RS, knit on WS

O yo

◫ k2tog on RS, p2tog on WS

◫ ssk on RS, ssp on WS

⅄ sk2p

V sl 1 purlwise with yarn in back on RS

◪ C1R [see Special abbreviations]

◪ C1L [see Special abbreviations]

◪ C2R [see Special abbreviations]

◪ C2L [see Special abbreviations]

☐ pattern repeat

| marker placement

Left pattern

56-stitch repeat

RIGHT PATTERN

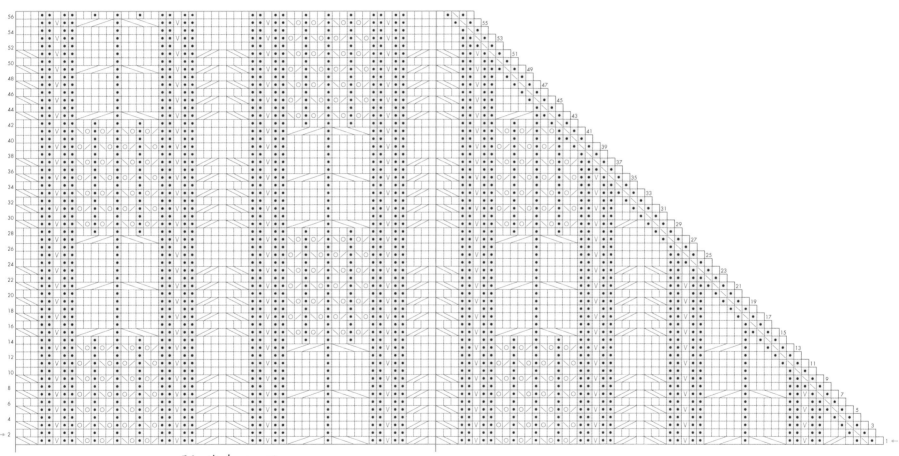

56-stitch repeat

End pattern

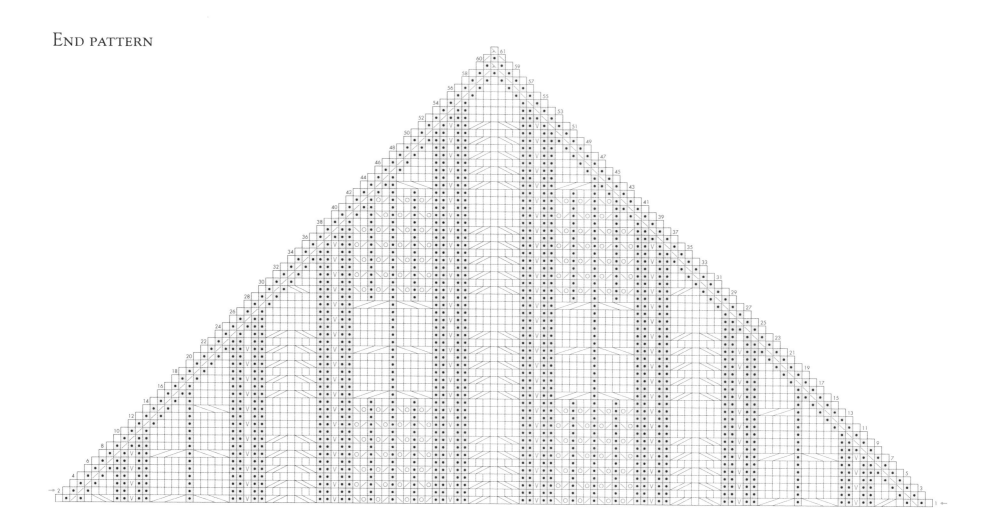

NETTLE

Finished measurements

72" [183 cm] wingspan and 23" [58.5 cm] deep at center

Yarn

Sparrow by Quince & Co
(100% organic linen; 168yd [155m]/50g)
• 4 skeins Truffle 211

Needles

• One 32" circular needle in size US 5 [3.75 mm]
Or size to obtain gauge

Notions

• Stitch markers
• Tapestry needle
• Blocking pins and wires

Gauge

18 sts and 24 rows = 4" [10 cm] in eyelet pattern, after blocking.

Special abbreviations

yo2: Bring yarn over needle twice. On the next row, knit into the first yarn over, then purl the second yarn over (1 stitch increased).

Eyelet pattern for swatching (mult of 4 sts +1)

Row 1: (RS) K1, *yo, s2kp, yo, k1; rep from * to end.
Row 2: Purl.
Row 3: K2tog, yo, *k1, yo, s2kp, yo; rep from * to last 3 sts, k1, yo, ssk.
Row 4: Purl.
Repeat Rows 1-4 for eyelet pattern for swatching.

Notes

1. Nettle is knitted flat, beginning at wide top edge and decreasing at each side edge every row to bottom point.

2. Take care that yarnovers remain on the correct side of stitch markers.
3. Before blocking, the shawl tips will appear unbalanced. This is due to the bias caused by the stitch pattern and the single-ply yarn. Blocking pins and wires are required not only to open up lace pattern, but to relieve this bias and give the shawl symmetry.

SHAWL

Using the long-tail cast on, CO 307 sts. Do not join.
First row place markers: (WS) P2tog, p137, place marker for panel (pm), p28, pm for panel, p138 sts to last 2 sts, ssp (2 sts dec'd)—305 sts rem.

Begin panel and eyelet pattern

See also main chart, page 118.
Decreases occur every row throughout shawl.
Row 1: (RS) K1, s2kp, yo, k1, (yo, s2kp, yo, k1) to 2 sts before marker (m), yo, sl 2 sts tog knitwise, remove m, k1, pass 2 sl sts over, pm, yo, (k1, yo, s2kp, yo) two times, k2tog, k1, yo2, s2kp, yo2, k1, ssk, (yo, s2kp, yo, k1) two times, yo, sl 2 sts tog knitwise, remove m, k1, pass 2 sl sts over, pm, yo, k1, (yo, s2kp, yo, k1) to last 4 sts, yo, s2kp, k1 (2 sts dec'd)—303 sts rem.
Row 2: P2tog, purl to yo2, (k1, p1) into yo2, p1, (k1, p1) into yo2, purl to last 2 sts, ssp (2 sts dec'd)—301 sts rem.
Row 3: K1, s2kp, yo, k1, (yo, s2kp, yo, k1) to m, slip marker (sl m), yo, s2kp, yo, k1, yo, s2kp, yo, k3tog, (yo, k1) two times, yo, s2kp, yo, (k1, yo) two times, sssk, (yo, s2kp, yo, k1) two times to m, sl m, (yo, s2kp, yo, k1) to last 4 sts, yo, s2kp, k1—299 sts rem.
Row 4 and all further WS rows unless specified: P2tog, purl to last 2 sts, ssp (2 sts dec'd).

Row 5: K1, s2kp, yo, k1, (yo, s2kp, yo, k1) to 2 sts before m, yo, sl 2 sts tog knitwise, remove m, k1, pass 2 sl sts over, pm, yo, k1, yo, s2kp, yo, k3tog, (k1, yo) two times, k2, yo, s2kp, yo, k2, (yo, k1) two times, sssk, yo, s2kp, yo, k1, yo, sl 2 sts tog knitwise, remove m, k1, pass 2 sl sts over, pm, yo, k1, (yo, s2kp, yo, k1) to last 4 sts, yo, s2kp, k1—295 sts rem.

Row 7: K1, s2kp, yo, k1, (yo, s2kp, yo, k1) to m, sl m, yo, s2kp, yo, k3tog, k2, yo, k1, yo, k3, yo, s2kp, yo, k3, yo, k1, yo, k2, sssk, yo, s2kp, yo, k1, sl m, (yo, s2kp, yo, k1) to last 4 sts, yo, s2kp, k1—291 sts rem.

Row 9: K1, s2kp, yo, k1, (yo, s2kp, yo, k1) to 2 sts before m, yo, sl 2 sts tog knitwise, remove m, k1, pass 2 sl sts over, pm, yo, ssk, yo, k9, yo, s2kp, yo, k9, yo, k2tog, yo, sl 2 sts tog knitwise, remove m, k1, pass 2 sl sts over, pm, yo, k1, (yo, s2kp, yo, k1) to last 4 sts, yo, s2kp, k1—287 sts rem.

Row 11: K1, s2kp, yo, k1, (yo, s2kp, yo, k1) to m, sl m, yo, s2kp, yo, k7, k2tog, yo2, s2kp, yo2, ssk, k7, yo, s2kp, yo, k1, sl m, (yo, s2kp, yo, k1) to last 4 sts, yo, s2kp, k1—283 sts rem.

Row 12: (WS) P2tog, purl to yo2, (k1, p1) into yo2, p1, (k1, p1) into yo2, purl to last 2 sts, ssp—281 sts rem.

Row 13: K1, s2kp, yo, k1, (yo, s2kp, yo, k1) to 2 sts before m, yo, sl 2 sts tog knitwise, remove m, k1, pass 2 sl sts over, pm, yo, ssk, yo, k5, k2tog, yo2, s2kp, yo, k1, yo, s2kp, yo2, ssk, k5, yo, k2tog, yo, sl 2 sts tog knitwise, remove m, k1, pass 2 sl sts over, pm, yo, k1, (yo, s2kp, yo, k1) to last 4 sts, yo, s2kp, k1—279 sts rem.

Row 14: (WS) P2tog, purl to yo2, (k1, p1) into yo2, p5, (k1, p1) into yo2, purl to last 2 sts, ssp—277 sts rem.

Row 15: K1, s2kp, yo, k1, (yo, s2kp, yo, k1) to m, sl m, yo, s2kp, yo, k3, k2tog, yo2, (s2kp, yo, k1, yo) two times, s2kp, yo2, ssk, k3, yo, s2kp, yo, k1, sl m, (yo, s2kp, yo, k1) to last 4 sts, yo, s2kp, k1—275 sts rem.

Row 16: (WS) P2tog, purl to yo2, (k1, p1) into yo2, p9, (k1, p1) into yo2, purl to last 2 sts, ssp—273 sts rem.

Row 17: K1, s2kp, yo, k1, (yo, s2kp, yo, k1) to 2 sts before m, yo, sl 2 sts tog knitwise, remove m, k1, pass 2 sl sts over, pm, yo, ssk, yo, k1, k2tog, yo2, s2kp, yo, (k1, yo, s2kp, yo) two times, k1, yo, s2kp, yo2, ssk, k1, yo, k2tog, yo, sl 2 sts tog knitwise, remove m, k1, pass 2 sl sts over, pm, yo, k1, (yo, s2kp, yo, k1) to last 4 sts, yo, s2kp, k1—271 sts rem.

Row 18: (WS) P2tog, purl to yo2, (k1, p1) into yo2, p13, (k1, p1) into yo2, purl to last 2 sts, ssp—269 sts rem.

Row 19: K1, s2kp, yo, k1, *yo, s2kp, yo, k1; rep from * to last 4 sts, yo, s2kp, k1—267 sts rem.

Row 20: (WS) P2tog, purl to last 2 sts, ssp—265 sts rem.

Rep Rows 1-20 five more times—65 sts rem.

Work Rows 1-8 one more time, removing panel markers on final row—49 sts rem.

Begin panel end

See also end chart, next page.

Row 1: (RS) K1, s2kp, yo, (k1, yo, s2kp, yo) two times, ssk, yo, k9, yo, s2kp, yo, k9, yo, k2tog, (yo, s2kp, yo, k1) two times, yo, s2kp, k1 (2 sts dec'd)—47 sts rem.

Row 2: P2tog, purl to last 2 sts, ssp (2 sts dec'd)—45 sts rem.

Row 3: K1, s2kp, yo, (k1, yo, s2kp, yo) two times, k7, k2tog, yo2, s2kp, yo2, ssk, k7, (yo, s2kp, yo, k1) two times, yo, s2kp, k1—43 sts rem.

Row 4: P2tog, purl to yo2, (k1, p1) into yo2, p1, (k1, p1) into yo2, purl to last 2 sts, ssp—41 sts rem.

Row 5: K1, s2kp, yo, k1, yo, s2kp, yo, ssk, yo, k5, k2tog, yo2, s2kp, yo, k1, yo, s2kp, yo2, ssk, k5, yo, k2tog, yo, s2kp, yo, k1, yo, s2kp, k1—39 sts rem.

Row 6: P2tog, purl to yo2, (k1, p1) into yo2, p5, (k1, p1) into yo2, purl to last 2 sts, ssp—37 sts rem.

Row 7: K1, s2kp, yo, k1, yo, s2kp, yo, k3, k2tog, yo2, s2kp, yo, k1, yo, s2kp, yo, k1, yo, s2kp, yo2, ssk, k3, yo, s2kp, yo, k1, yo, s2kp, k1—35 sts rem.

Row 8: P2tog, purl to yo2, (k1, p1) into yo2, p9, (k1, p1) into yo2, purl to last 2 sts, ssp—33 sts rem.

Row 9: K1, s2kp, yo, ssk, yo, k1, k2tog, yo2, s2kp, yo, (k1, yo, s2kp, yo) two times, k1, yo, s2kp, yo2, ssk, k1, yo, k2tog, yo, s2kp, k1—31 sts rem.

Row 10: P2tog, purl to yo2, (k1, p1) into yo2, p13, (k1, p1) into yo2, purl to last 2 sts, ssp—29 sts rem.

Row 11: K1, s2kp, yo, *k1, yo, s2kp, yo; rep from * to last 5 sts, k1, yo, s2kp, k1—27 sts rem.

Row 12 and all further WS rows unless specified: P2tog, purl to last 2 sts, ssp—25 sts rem.

Rows 13-18: Rep Rows 11 and 12 three times—13 sts rem.

Row 19: (RS) K1, s2kp, yo, k1, yo, s2kp, yo, k1, yo, s2kp, k1—11 sts rem.

Row 21: K1, s2kp, yo, k1, yo, s2kp, k1—7 sts rem.

Row 23: K1, s2kp, k1—3 sts rem.

Row 24: (WS) P3tog—1 st rem.

Cut yarn and draw through rem st.

Finishing

Weave in ends. Wet block shawl to finished measurements, using blocking pins and wires.

KEY

- ☐ knit on RS, purl on WS
- • purl on RS, knit on WS
- ⋀ s2kp
- ⋀ sl 2 sts tog knitwise, remove m, k1, pass 2 sl sts over, pm
- ○ yo
- ○○ yo2
- ╱ k2tog on RS, p2tog on WS
- ╲ ssk on RS, ssp on WS
- ⪤ k3tog on RS, p3tog on WS
- ⪥ sssk
- ☐ pattern repeat
- | marker placement

END PATTERN

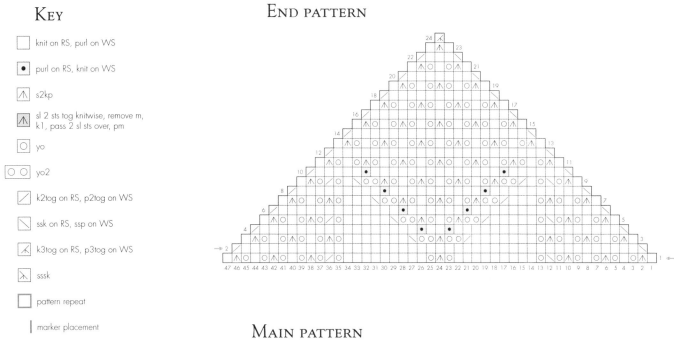

MAIN PATTERN

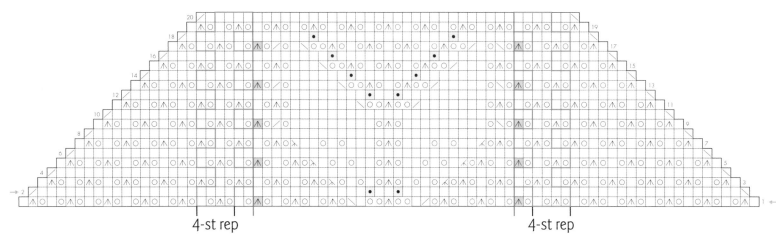

4-st rep   4-st rep

118

DATURA

Finished measurements

76" [193 cm] wingspan and 40" [101.5 cm] deep at center

Yarn

Phoebe by Quince & Co
(100% extrafine American merino; 301 yd [275m]/100g)

- 5 skeins Jupiter 805

Needles

- One 32" circular needle in size US 7 [4.5 mm]

Or size to obtain gauge

Notions

- Stitch markers
- Cable needle (optional)
- Tapestry needle

Gauge

17 sts and 34 rows = 4" [10 cm] in garter stitch, after blocking.

Special abbreviations

LPC-tbl: Slip 1 stitch onto cable needle (cn) and hold in front, p1, then k1-tbl from cn.

RPC-tbl: Slip 1 stitch onto cn and hold in back, k1-tbl, then p1 from cn.

Note

Datura is knitted flat, from the bottom up, with decreases every RS row at each side edge and at center spine throughout shawl.

SHAWL

Using the long-tail cast on, CO 221 sts, place marker for center, CO 221 more sts—442 sts on needle. Do not join.

Begin garter trim and shawl decreases

Decreases occur every RS row throughout shawl.

First row *dec row:* (RS) K2, ssk, knit to 2 sts before marker (m), k2tog, slip marker (sl m), ssk, knit to last 4 sts, k2tog, k2 (4 sts dec'd)—438 sts rem.

Next row: Knit.

Rep the last 2 rows nine more times—402 sts rem.

Begin border pattern

See also chart, page 123.

Note: Two stitches in garter stitch at each end of shawl are not included in the chart.

Row 1: (RS) K2, *ssk, (k1, yo, ssk) two times, k3, k2tog, yo, (k1, k2tog, yo) two times, [(k1, yo, ssk) three times, k3, (k2tog, yo, k1) two times, k2tog, yo] eight times, (k1, yo, ssk) three times, k3, (k2tog, yo, k1) two times, k2tog; sl m for center and rep from * one more time, k2 (4 sts dec'd)—398 sts rem.

Row 2: K2, *p18, k1, (p19, k1) eight times, p18; sl m for center and rep from * one more time, k2.

Row 3: K2, *ssk, (k1, yo, ssk) two times, k1, (k2tog, yo, k1) three times, [p1, (k1, yo, ssk) three times, k1, (k2tog, yo, k1) three times] eight times, p1, (k1, yo, ssk) three times, k1, (k2tog, yo, k1) two times, k2tog; sl m for center and rep from * one more time, k2—394 sts rem.

Row 4: K2, *p16, k2, (k1, p17, k2) eight times, k1, p16; sl m for center and rep from * one more time, k2.

Row 5: K2, *(ssk, k1, yo) two times, s2kp, yo, (k1, k2tog, yo) two times, k1, p1, [p2, (k1, yo, ssk) two times, k1, yo, s2kp, yo, (k1, k2tog, yo) two times, k1, p1] eight times, p2, (k1, yo, ssk) two times, k1, yo, s2kp, (yo, k1, k2tog) two times; sl m for center and rep from * one more time, k2—390 sts rem.
Row 6: K2, *p14, k3, (k2, p15, k3) eight times, k2, p14; sl m for center and rep from * one more time, k2.
Row 7: K2, *ssk, k1, yo, ssk, k3, (k2tog, yo, k1) two times, p2, [k1-tbl, p2, (k1, yo, ssk) two times, k3, (k2tog, yo, k1) two times, p2] eight times, k1-tbl, p2, (k1, yo, ssk) two times, k3, k2tog, yo, k1, k2tog; sl m for center and rep from * one more time, k2—386 sts rem.
Row 8: K2, *p12, k3, p1-tbl, (k3, p13, k3, p1-tbl) eight times, k3, p12; sl m for center and rep from * one more time, k2.
Row 9: K2, *ssk, k1, yo, ssk, k1, (k2tog, yo, k1) two times, p3, [k1-tbl, p3, (k1, yo, ssk) two times, k1, (k2tog, yo, k1) two times, p3] eight times, k1-tbl, p3, (k1, yo, ssk) two times, k1, k2tog, yo, k1, k2tog; sl m for center and rep from * one more time, k2—382 sts rem.
Row 10: K2, *p10, k2, p1-tbl, k1, p1-tbl, (k1, p1-tbl, k2, p11, k2, p1-tbl, k1, p1-tbl) eight times, k1, p1-tbl, k2, p10; sl m for center and rep from * one more time, k2.
Row 11: K2, *ssk, k1, yo, s2kp, yo, k1, k2tog, yo, k1, p2, LPC-tbl, (k1-tbl, RPC-tbl, p2, k1, yo, ssk, k1, yo, s2kp, yo, k1, k2tog, yo, k1, p2, LPC-tbl) eight times, k1-tbl, RPC-tbl, p2, k1, yo, ssk, k1, yo, s2kp, yo, k1, k2tog; sl m for center and rep from * one more time, k2—378 sts rem.

Row 12: K2, *p8, k2, p1-tbl, k1, (p1-tbl) two times, [p1-tbl, k1, p1-tbl, k2, p9, k2, p1-tbl, k1, (p1-tbl) two times] eight times, p1-tbl, k1, p1-tbl, k2, p8; sl m for center and rep from * one more time, k2.
Row 13: K2, *ssk, k3, k2tog, yo, k1, p2, LPC-tbl, p1, (k1-tbl, p1, RPC-tbl, p2, k1, yo, ssk, k3, k2tog, yo, k1, p2, LPC-tbl, p1) eight times, k1-tbl, p1, RPC-tbl, p2, k1, yo, ssk, k3, k2tog; sl m, for center and rep from * one more time, k2—374 sts rem.
Row 14: K2, *p6, k4, p1-tbl, k1, p1-tbl, (k1, p1-tbl, k4, p7, k4, p1-tbl, k1, p1-tbl) eight times, k1, p1-tbl, k4, p6; sl m for center and rep from * one more time, k2.
Row 15: K2, *ssk, k1, k2tog, yo, k1, p4, LPC-tbl, (k1-tbl, RPC-tbl, p4, k1, yo, ssk, k1, k2tog, yo, k1, p4, LPC-tbl) eight times, k1-tbl, RPC-tbl, p4, k1, yo, ssk, k1, k2tog; sl m for center and rep from * one more time, k2—370 sts rem.
Row 16: K2, *p4, k6, (p1-tbl) two times, [p1-tbl, k6, p5, k6, (p1-tbl) two times] eight times, p1-tbl, k6, p4; sl m for center and rep from * one more time, k2.
Row 17: K2, *s2kp, yo, k1, p7, (k1-tbl, p7, k1, yo, s2kp, yo, k1, p7) eight times, k1-tbl, p7, k1, yo, s2kp; sl m for center and rep from * one more time, k2—366 sts rem.
Row 18: K2, *p3, k6, (p1-tbl) two times, [p1-tbl, k6, p5, k6, (p1-tbl) two times] eight times, p1-tbl, k6, p3; sl m for center and rep from * one more time, k2.
Row 19: K2, *ssk, yo, ssk, p4, RPC-tbl, (k1-tbl, LPC-tbl, p4, k2tog, yo, k3, yo, ssk, p4, RPC-tbl) eight times, k1-tbl, LPC-tbl, p4, k2tog, yo, k2tog; sl m for center and rep from * one more time, k2—362 sts rem.

Row 20: K2, *p3, k4, p1-tbl, k1, p1-tbl, (k1, p1-tbl, k4, p7, k4, p1-tbl, k1, p1-tbl) eight times, k1, p1-tbl, k4, p3; sl m for center and rep from * one more time, k2.
Row 21: K2, *ssk, yo, ssk, p2, RPC-tbl, p1, (k1-tbl, p1, LPC-tbl, p2, k2tog, yo, k5, yo, ssk, p2, RPC-tbl, p1) eight times, k1-tbl, p1, LPC-tbl, p2, k2tog, yo, k2tog; sl m for center and rep from * one more time, k2—358 sts rem.
Row 22: K2, *p3, k2, p1-tbl, k1, (p1-tbl) two times, [p1-tbl, k1, p1-tbl, k2, p9, k2, p1-tbl, k1, (p1-tbl) two times] eight times, p1-tbl, k1, p1-tbl, k2, p3; sl m for center and rep from * one more time, k2.
Row 23: K2, *ssk, yo, ssk, p2, RPC-tbl, [k1-tbl, LPC-tbl, p2, (k2tog, yo, k1) two times, yo, ssk, k1, yo, ssk, p2, RPC-tbl] eight times, k1-tbl, LPC-tbl, p2, k2tog, yo, k2tog; sl m for center and rep from * one more time, k2—354 sts rem.
Row 24: K2, *p3, k2, p1-tbl, k1, p1-tbl, (k1, p1-tbl, k2, p11, k2, p1-tbl, k1, p1-tbl) eight times, k1, p1-tbl, k2, p3; sl m for center and rep from * one more time, k2.
Row 25: K2, *ssk, yo, ssk, p3, (k1-tbl, p3, k2tog, yo, k1, k2tog, yo, k3, yo, ssk, k1, yo, ssk, p3) eight times, k1-tbl, p3, k2tog, yo, k2tog; sl m for center and rep from * one more time, k2—350 sts rem.
Row 26: K2, *p3, k3, p1-tbl, (k3, p13, k3, p1-tbl) eight times, k3, p3; sl m for center and rep from * one more time, k2.
Row 27: K2, *ssk, yo, ssk, p2, (k1-tbl, p2, k2tog, yo, k1, k2tog, yo, k5, yo, ssk, k1, yo, ssk, p2) eight times, k1-tbl, p2, k2tog, yo, k2tog; sl m for center and rep from * one more time, k2—346 sts rem.

Row 28: K2, *p3, k3, (k2, p15, k3) eight times, k2, p3; sl m for center and rep from * one more time, k2.

Row 29: K2, *ssk, yo, ssk, p1, [p2, (k2tog, yo, k1) three times, yo, ssk, (k1, yo, ssk) two times, p1] eight times, p2, k2tog, yo, k2tog; sl m for center and rep from * one more time, k2—342 sts rem.

Row 30: K2, *p3, k2, (k1, p17, k2) eight times, k1, p3; sl m for center and rep from * one more time, k2.

Row 31: K2, *ssk, yo, ssk, [p1, (k2tog, yo, k1) two times, k2tog, yo, k3, (yo, ssk, k1) two times, yo, ssk] eight times, p1, k2tog, yo, k2tog; sl m for center and rep from * one more time, k2—338 sts rem.

Row 32: K2, *p3, k1, (p19, k1) eight times, p3; sl m for center and rep from * one more time, k2.

Continue in garter stitch

Next row dec row: (RS) K2, ssk, knit to 2 sts before m, k2tog, sl m, ssk, knit to last 4 sts, k2tog, k2 (4 sts dec'd)—334 sts rem.

Next row: Knit.

Rep the last 2 rows 81 more times—10 sts rem.

Next row: (RS) K2, s2kp, remove m, s2kp, k2 (4 sts dec'd)—6 sts rem.

Next row: (WS) Bind off knitwise.

Finishing

Weave in ends. Wet block shawl to finished measurements.

KEY

☐	knit on RS, purl on WS
•	purl on RS, knit on WS
O	yo
╱	k2tog
╲	ssk
⋀	s2kp
ℓ	k1-tbl on RS, p1-tbl on WS
	LPC-tbl [see Special abbreviations]
	RPC-tbl [see Special abbreviations]
☐	pattern repeat

BORDER PATTERN

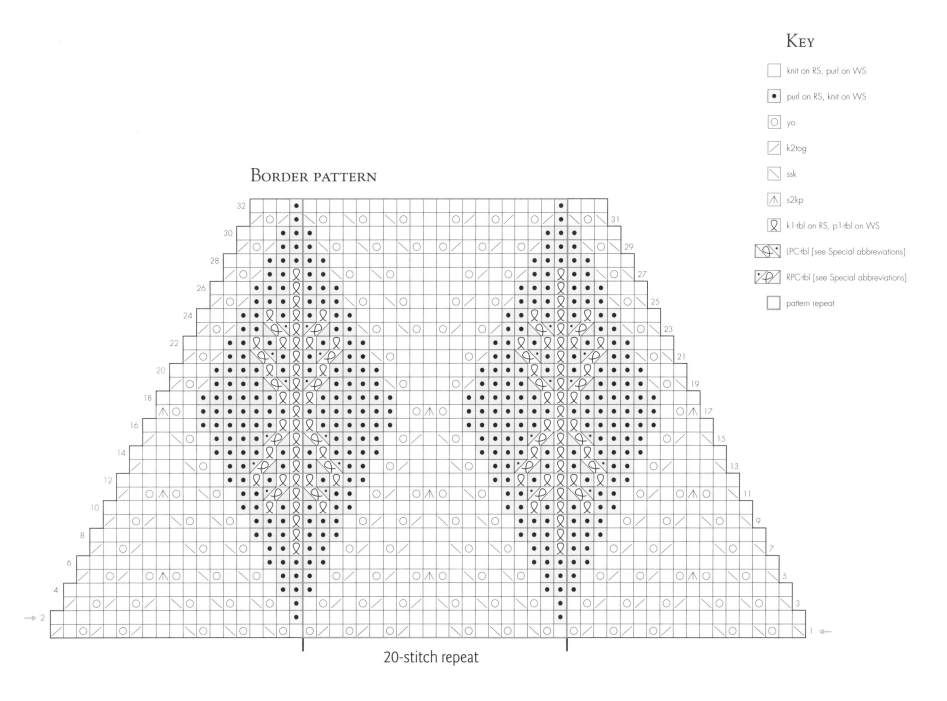

20-stitch repeat

Mugwort

Finished measurements

71" [180.5 cm] wingspan and 24" [61 cm] deep at center

Yarn

Owl by Quince & Co

(50% American wool, 50% alpaca; 120yd [110m]/50g)

- 7 skeins Cielo 318

Needles

- One 32" circular needle in size US 9 [5.5 mm]

Or size to obtain gauge

Notions

- Cable needle (optional)
- Tapestry needle

Gauge

24 sts and 28 rows = 4" [10 cm] in stitch pattern, after blocking.

Special abbreviations

make rickrack: (RS) Insert RH needle tip knitwise into the front leg of the second stitch on LH needle, but keep needle tip in front of the first stitch you've skipped. Wrap yarn around needle and draw through to make a new stitch, but do not drop any stitches from either needle. Insert RH needle tip knitwise into the front leg of the first stitch on LH needle and knit it. Drop both stitches from LH needle.

(WS) With yarn in front of work, bring RH needle tip to back of work, skip the first stitch (keeping needle tip behind first stitch) and insert RH needle tip purlwise (as if to purl through the back loop) into the back leg of the second stitch on RH needle. Wrap yarn around needle and draw through to make a new stitch, but do not drop any stitches from either needle. Insert RH needle tip purlwise into the front leg of the first stitch on LH needle and purl it. Drop both stitches from LH needle.

C4B (cable 4 back, leans to the right): Slip 2 stitches onto cable needle (cn) and hold in back, k2, then k2 from cn.

C4F (cable 4 front, leans to the left): Slip 2 stitches onto cn and hold in front, k2, then k2 from cn.

C4B-p (cross 2 knit over 2 purl right): Slip 2 stitches onto cn and hold in back, k2, then p2 from cn.

C4F-p (cross 2 knit over 2 purl left): Slip 2 stitches onto cn and hold in front, p2, then k2 from cn.

Stitch pattern for swatching (mult of 30 sts + 10)

Row 1: (RS) *(P1, make rickrack) three times, p1, k2, p4, C4B, C4F, p4, k2; rep from * to last 10 sts, (p1, make rickrack) three times, p1.

Row 2: (K1, make rickrack) three times, k1, *p2, k4, p8, k4, p2, k1, (make rickrack, k1) three times; rep from * to end.

Row 3: *(P1, make rickrack) three times, p1, C4F-p, C4B, k4, C4F, C4B-p; rep from * to last 10 sts, (p1, make rickrack) three times, p1.

Row 4: (K1, make rickrack) three times, k1, *k2, p16, k3, (make rickrack, k1) three times; rep from * to end.

Row 5: *(P1, make rickrack) three times, p3, C4B-p, C4B, C4F, C4F-p, p2; rep from * to last 10 sts, (p1, make rickrack) three times, p1.

Row 6: (K1, make rickrack) three times, k1, *k2, p2, k2, p8, k2, p2, k3, (make rickrack, k1) three times; rep from * to end.

Row 7: *(P1, make rickrack) three times, p1, C4B-p, p2, k8, p2, C4F-p; rep from * to last 10 sts, (p1, make rickrack) three times, p1.

Row 8: (K1, make rickrack) three times, k1, *p2, k4, p8, k4, p2, k1, (make rickrack, k1) three times; rep from * to end.

Repeat Rows 1-8 for stitch pattern for swatching.

Notes

1. Mugwort is knitted flat, from the bottom up, beginning at wide lower edge and decreased at each side edge every row and at center spine every RS row to center of back neck.
2. Due to the large size of the pattern motif, this pattern is charted only, broken into 20-row sections. Stitch counts are provided in the written pattern at the beginning and end of each section.
3. In order to make these large charts as small as possible, the stitch pattern repeat will shift at the beginning of each new chart. If you use markers to keep track of repeats, remove them as you go on the final WS row of each chart, then replace them according to the repeat while working Row 1 of the next chart.

Shawl

Using the long-tail cast on, CO 430 sts.

Begin Chart A

See chart A, next page.
Set up row: (WS) Work set up row of Chart A to end.
Next row: (RS) Work Row 1 of Chart A to end (4 sts dec'd)—426 sts rem.
Next row: Work Row 2 of chart to end (2 sts dec'd)—424 sts rem.
Work Rows 3-18 of Chart A—376 sts rem.

Begin Chart B

See chart B, next page.
Next row: (RS) Work Row 1 of Chart B to end (4 sts dec'd)—372 sts rem.
Next row: Work Row 2 of chart to end (2 sts dec'd)—370 sts rem.
Work Rows 3-20 of Chart B—316 sts rem.

Begin Chart C

See chart C, page 127.
Next row: (RS) Work Row 1 of Chart C to end (4 sts dec'd)—312 sts rem.
Next row: Work Row 2 of chart to end (2 sts dec'd)—310 sts rem.
Work Rows 3-20 of Chart C—256 sts rem.

Begin Chart D

See chart D, page 127.
Next row: (RS) Work Row 1 of Chart D to end (4 sts dec'd)—252 sts rem.
Next row: Work Row 2 of chart to end (2 sts dec'd)—250 sts rem.
Work Rows 3-20 of Chart D—196 sts rem.

Begin Chart E

See chart E, page 127.
Next row: (RS) Work Row 1 of Chart E to end (4 sts dec'd)—192 sts rem.
Next row: Work Row 2 of chart to end (2 sts dec'd)—190 sts rem.
Work Rows 3-20 of Chart E—136 sts rem.

Begin Chart F

See chart F, page 128.
Note: Only one complete repeat of stitch pattern now remains.
Next row: (RS) Work Row 1 of Chart F to end (4 sts dec'd)—132 sts rem.
Next row: Work Row 2 of chart to end (2 sts dec'd)—130 sts rem.
Work Rows 3-20 of Chart F—76 sts rem.

Begin Chart G

See chart G, page 128.
Note: Final pattern repeat will now be decreased to end.
Next row: (RS) Work Row 1 of Chart G to end (4 sts dec'd)—72 sts rem.
Next row: Work Row 2 of chart to end (2 sts dec'd)—70 sts rem.
Work Rows 3-25 of Chart G—2 sts rem.
Bring the first st on RH needle up and over second to BO 1 st.
Break yarn and draw through rem st.

Finishing

Weave in ends. Wet block shawl to finished measurements.

Chart B

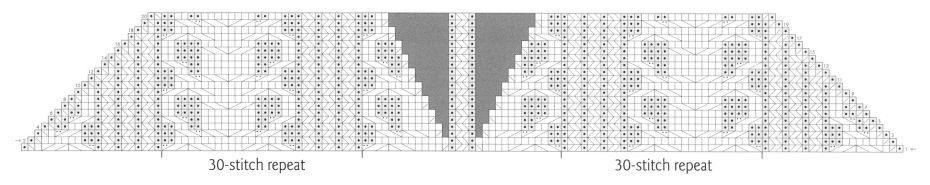

30-stitch repeat   30-stitch repeat

Chart A

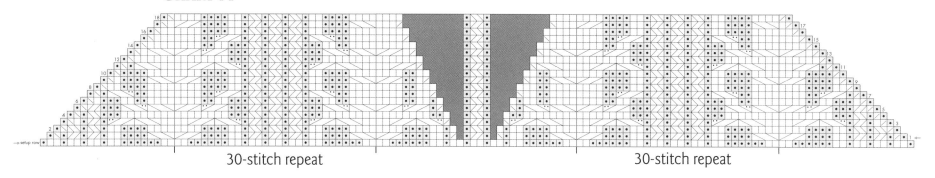

30-stitch repeat   30-stitch repeat

Key

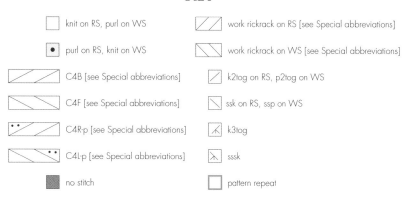

☐ knit on RS, purl on WS	⟋ work rickrack on RS [see Special abbreviations]
⊡ purl on RS, knit on WS	⟍ work rickrack on WS [see Special abbreviations]
⟋ C4B [see Special abbreviations]	⟋ k2tog on RS, p2tog on WS
⟍ C4F [see Special abbreviations]	⟍ ssk on RS, ssp on WS
•• ⟋ C4R-p [see Special abbreviations]	⟋ k3tog
⟍ •• C4L-p [see Special abbreviations]	⟍ sssk
■ no stitch	☐ pattern repeat

Chart E

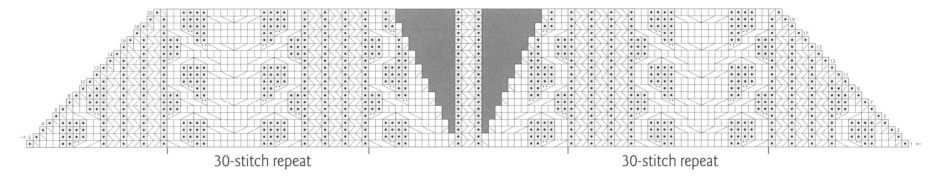

30-stitch repeat   30-stitch repeat

Chart D

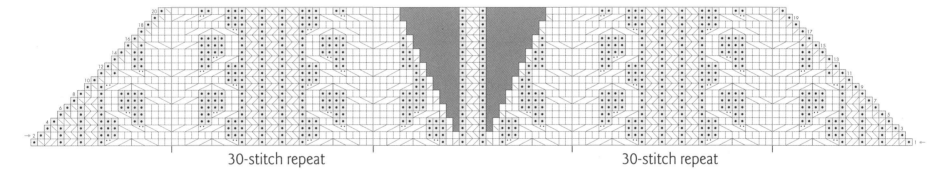

30-stitch repeat   30-stitch repeat

Chart C

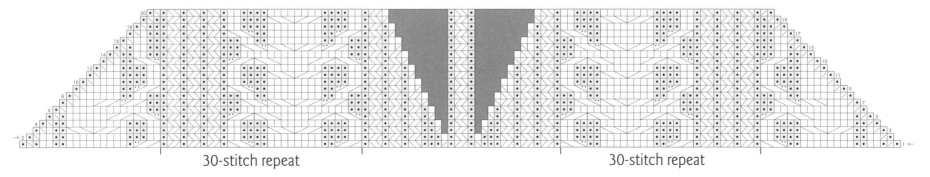

30-stitch repeat   30-stitch repeat

Chart G

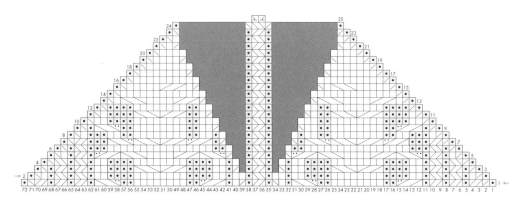

Chart F

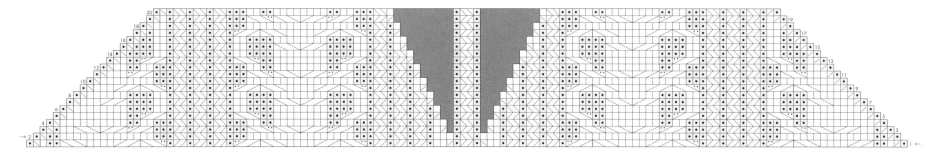

MOONFLOWER

Finished measurements
71″ [180.5 cm] wingspan and 36″ [91.5 cm] deep at center

Yarn
Owl by Quince & Co
(50% American wool, 50% alpaca; 120yd [110m]/50g)
- 8 skeins Tyto 301

Needles
- One 32″ circular needle in size US 9 [5.5 mm]

Or size to obtain gauge

Notions
- Stitch marker
- Locking stitch markers
- Tapestry needle

Gauge
16 sts and 32 rows = 4″ [10 cm] in garter stitch, after blocking.

Special abbreviations
sl: Slip 1 stitch purlwise with yarn to the WS.
dbl-dec: Slip next stitch purlwise, k2tog the yo and stitch after gap, then pass slipped stitch over (2 stitches decreased).

Note
Moonflower's border is knitted flat, from side to side, with yarnover short rows shaping the left and right tips and the mitered corner at the center. Stitches are picked up along side of border and worked in garter stitch, decreasing at each side edge and at center spine every RS row to center of back neck.

SHAWL
Using the long-tail cast on, CO 36 sts. Do not join.

Begin left border tip
Border tip is shaped using yarnover short rows.
See also left border tip chart, page 134.
Short row 1: (RS) K3, turn; (WS) yo, k3.
Short row 2: (RS) K3, k2tog (the yo and st after gap), turn; (WS) yo, k4.
Short row 3: (RS) K4, p2tog (the yo and st after gap), turn; (WS) yo, k5.
Short row 4: (RS) K4, p1, k2tog, turn; (WS) yo, p1, k5.
Short row 5: (RS) K4, p1, sl 1, p2tog, turn; (WS) yo, k1, p1, k5.
Short row 6: (RS) K4, p1, sl 1, p1, k2tog, turn; (WS) yo, p1, k1, p1, k5.
Short row 7: (RS) K4, p1, sl 1, p1, k1, k2tog, turn; (WS) yo, p2, k1, p1, k5.
Short row 8: (RS) K4, p1, sl 1, p1, k1, yo, dbl-dec, turn; (WS) yo, p3, k1, p1, k5.
Short row 9: (RS) K4, p1, sl 1, p1, k2, yo, dbl-dec, turn; (WS) yo, p4, k1, p1, k5.
Short row 10: (RS) K4, p1, sl 1, p1, k3, yo, dbl-dec, turn; (WS) yo, p5, k1, p1, k5.
Short row 11: (RS) K4, p1, sl 1, p1, k4, yo, dbl-dec, turn; (WS) yo, p6, k1, p1, k5.
Short row 12: (RS) K4, p1, sl 1, p1, k5, yo, dbl-dec, turn; (WS) yo, p7, k1, p1, k5.
Short row 13: (RS) K4, p1, sl 1, p1, k6, yo, dbl-dec, turn; (WS) yo, p8, k1, p1, k5.
Short row 14: (RS) K4, p1, sl 1, p1, (k1, p1) three times, k2tog, yo, k2tog, turn; (WS) yo, p3, (k1, p1) four times, k5.

Short row 15: (RS) K4, p1, sl 1, p2, (k1, p1) two times, k2tog, yo, k2, p2tog, turn; (WS) yo, k1, p4, (k1, p1) two times, k2, p1, k5.

Short row 16: (RS) K4, p1, sl 1, p1, (k1, p1) two times, k2tog, yo, k3, p1, k2tog, turn; (WS) yo, p1, k1, p5, (k1, p1) three times, k5.

Short row 17: (RS) K4, p1, sl 1, p2, k1, p1, k2tog, yo, k4, p1, sl 1, p2tog, turn; (WS) yo, k1, p1, k1, p6, k1, p1, k2, p1, k5.

Short row 18: (RS) K4, p1, sl 1, p1, k1, p1, k2tog, yo, k5, p1, sl 1, p1, k2tog, turn; (WS) yo, (p1, k1) two times, p7, (k1, p1) two times, k5.

Short row 19: (RS) K4, p1, sl 1, p2, k2tog, yo, k6, p1, sl 1, p1, k1, k2tog, turn; (WS) yo, p2, k1, p1, k1, p8, k2, p1, k5.

Short row 20: (RS) K4, p1, sl 1, p1, k1, yo, ssk, (p1, k1) three times, p1, sl 1, p1, k1, yo, dbl-dec, turn; (WS) yo, p3, (k1, p1) four times, k1, p3, k1, p1, k5.

Short row 21: (RS) K4, p1, sl 1, p1, k2, yo, ssk, (p1, k1) two times, p2, sl 1, p1, k2, yo, dbl-dec, turn; (WS) yo, p4, k1, p1, k2, (p1, k1) two times, p4, k1, p1, k5.

Short row 22: (RS) K4, p1, sl 1, p1, k3, yo, ssk, (p1, k1) two times, p1, sl 1, p1, k3, yo, dbl-dec, turn; (WS) yo, p5, (k1, p1) three times, k1, p5, k1, p1, k5.

Short row 23: (RS) K4, p1, sl 1, p1, k4, yo, ssk, p1, k1, p2, sl 1, p1, k4, yo, dbl-dec, turn; (WS) yo, p6, k1, p1, k2, p1, k1, p6, k1, p1, k5.

Short row 24: (RS) K4, p1, sl 1, p1, k5, yo, ssk, p1, k1, p1, sl 1, p1, k5, yo, dbl-dec, turn; (WS) yo, p7, (k1, p1) two times, k1, p7, k1, p1, k5.

Short row 25: (RS) K4, p1, sl 1, p1, k6, yo, ssk, p2, sl 1, p1, k6, yo, dbl-dec, turn; (WS) yo, p8, k1, p1, k2, p8, k1, p1, k5.

Short row 26: (RS) K4, p1, sl 1, p1, (k1, p1) three times, k2tog, yo, k1, p1, sl 1, p1, (k1, p1) three times, k2tog, yo, k2tog, turn; (WS) yo, p3, (k1, p1) four times, k1, p3, (k1, p1) four times, k5.

Short row 27: (RS) K4, *p1, sl 1, p2, (k1, p1) two times, k2tog, yo, k2; rep from * one more time, p2tog, turn; (WS) yo, k1, *p4, (k1, p1) two times, k2, p1, k1; rep from * one more time, k4.

Short row 28: (RS) K4, *p1, sl 1, p1, (k1, p1) two times, k2tog, yo, k3; rep from * one more time, p1, k2tog, turn; (WS) yo, p1, k1, *p5, (k1, p1) three times, k1; rep from * one more time, k4.

Short row 29: (RS) K4, *p1, sl 1, p2, k1, p1, k2tog, yo, k4; rep from * one more time, p1, sl 1, p2tog, turn; (WS) yo, k1, p1, k1, *p6, k1, p1, k2, p1, k1; rep from * one more time, k4.

Short row 30: (RS) K4, *p1, sl 1, p1, k1, p1, k2tog, yo, k5; rep from * one more time, p1, sl 1, p1, k2tog, turn; (WS) yo, k2, p1, k1, *p7, (k1, p1) two times, k1; rep from * one more time, k4.

Short row 31: (RS) K4, *p1, sl 1, p2, k2tog, yo, k6; rep from * one more time, p1, sl 1, p1, k1, k2tog, turn; (WS) yo, (k1, p1) two times, k1, *p8, k2, p1, k1; rep from * one more time, k4.

Row 32: (RS) K4, *p1, sl 1, p1, k1, yo, ssk, (p1, k1) three times; rep from * one more time, p1, sl 1, p1, k2, k2tog (resolving final short row), k2 sts to end. *Place a locking st marker at the end of this RS row.*

Row 33: (WS) K6, p1, k1, *(p1, k1) three times, p3, k1, p1, k1; rep from * one more time, k4.

Continue left border

See also main chart, page 134.

Row 1: (RS) K4, p1, *sl 1, p1, k2, yo, ssk, (p1, k1) two times, p2; rep from * one more time, sl 1, p1, k5.

Row 2: K6, p1, *k2, (p1, k1) two times, p4, k1, p1; rep from * one more time, k5.

Row 3: K4, p1, *sl 1, p1, k3, yo, ssk, (p1, k1) two times, p1; rep from * one more time, sl 1, p1, k5.

Row 4: K6, p1, *(k1, p1) two times, k1, p5, k1, p1; rep from * one more time, k5.

Row 5: K4, p1, *sl 1, p1, k4, yo, ssk, p1, k1, p2; rep from * one more time, sl 1, p1, k5.

Row 6: K6, p1, *k2, p1, k1, p6, k1, p1; rep from * one more time, k5.

Row 7: K4, p1, *sl 1, p1, k5, yo, ssk, p1, k1, p1; rep from * one more time, sl 1, p1, k5.

Row 8: K6, p1, *k1, p1, k1, p7, k1, p1; rep from * one more time, k5.

Row 9: K4, p1, *sl 1, p1, k6, yo, ssk, p2; rep from * one more time, sl 1, p1, k5.

Row 10: K6, p1, *k2, p8, k1, p1; rep from * one more time, k5.

Row 11: K4, p1, *sl 1, p1, (k1, p1) three times, k2tog, yo, k1, p1; rep from * one more time, sl 1, p1, k5.

Row 12: K6, p1, *k1, p3, (k1, p1) four times; rep from * one more time, k5.

Row 13: K4, p1, *sl 1, p2, (k1, p1) two times, k2tog, yo, k2, p1; rep from * one more time, sl 1, p1, k5.

Row 14: K6, p1, *k1, p4, (k1, p1) two times, k2, p1; rep from * one more time, k5.

Row 15: K4, p1, *sl 1, (p1, k1) two times, p1, k2tog, yo, k3, p1; rep from * one more time, sl 1, p1, k5.

Row 16: K6, p1, *k1, p5, (k1, p1) three times; rep from * one more time, k5.

Row 17: K4, p1, *sl 1, p2, k1, p1, k2tog, yo, k4, p1; rep from * one more time, sl 1, p1, k5.

Row 18: K6, p1, *k1, p6, k1, p1, k2, p1; rep from * one more time, k5.

Row 19: K4, p1, *sl 1, p1, k1, p1, k2tog, yo, k5, p1; rep from * one more time, sl 1, p1, k5.

Row 20: K6, p1, *k1, p7, (k1, p1) two times; rep from * one more time, k5.

Row 21: K4, p1, *sl 1, p2, k2tog, yo, k6, p1; rep from * one more time, sl 1, p1, k5.

Row 22: K6, p1, *k1, p8, k2, p1; rep from * one more time, k5.

Row 23: K4, p1, *sl 1, p1, k1, yo, ssk, (p1, k1) three times, p1; rep from * one more time, sl 1, p1, k5.

Row 24: K6, p1, *(k1, p1) three times, k1, p3, k1, p1; rep from * one more time, k5.

Rep the last 24 rows nine more times.

Begin left corner edge

The left corner of the mitered center builds a foundation of short rows that do not get resolved until working right corner.

See also left corner chart, page 135.

Short row 1: (RS) K4, *p1, sl 1, p1, k2, yo, ssk, (p1, k1) two times, p1; rep from * one more time, p1, sl 1, p1, k2, turn; (WS) yo, k3, p1, k1, *(k1, p1) two times, k1, p4, k1, p1, k1; rep from * one more time, k4.

Short row 2: (RS) K4, *p1, sl 1, p1, k3, yo, ssk, (p1, k1) two times; rep from * one more time, p1, sl 1, p1, k1, turn; (WS) yo, k2, p1, k1, *(p1, k1) two times, p5, k1, p1, k1; rep from * one more time, k4.

Short row 3: (RS) K4, *p1, sl 1, p1, k4, yo, ssk, p1, k1, p1; rep from * one more time, p1, sl 1, p1, turn; (WS) yo, k1, p1, k1, *k1, p1, k1, p6, k1, p1, k1; rep from * one more time, k4.

Short row 4: (RS) K4, *p1, sl 1, p1, k5, yo, ssk, p1, k1; rep from * one more time, p1, k1, turn; (WS) yo, p1, k1, *p1, k1, p7, k1, p1, k1; rep from * one more time, k4.

Short row 5: (RS) K4, *p1, sl 1, p1, k6, yo, ssk, p1; rep from * one more time, p1, turn; (WS) yo, k1, *k1, p8, k1, p1, k1; rep from * one more time, k4.

Short row 6: (RS) K4, *p1, sl 1, p1, (k1, p1) three times, k2tog, yo, k1; rep from * one more time, turn; (WS) yo, *p3, (k1, p1) four times, k1; rep from * one more time, k4.

Short row 7: (RS) K4, p1, sl 1, p2, (k1, p1) two times, k2tog, yo, k2, p1, sl 1, p2, (k1, p1) two times, k2tog, yo, k1, turn; (WS) yo, p3, (k1, p1) two times, k2, p1, k1, p4, (k1, p1) two times, k2, p1, k5.

Short row 8: (RS) K4, p1, sl 1, p1, (k1, p1) two times, k2tog, yo, k3, p1, sl 1, p1, (k1, p1) two times, k2tog, yo, k1, turn; (WS) yo, p3, (k1, p1) three times, k1, p5, (k1, p1) three times, k5.

Short row 9: (RS) K4, p1, sl 1, p2, k1, p1, k2tog, yo, k4, p1, sl 1, p2, k1, p1, k2tog, yo, k1, turn; (WS) yo, p3, k1, p1, k2, p1, k1, p6, k1, p1, k2, p1, k5.

Short row 10: (RS) K4, p1, sl 1, p1, k1, p1, k2tog, yo, k5, p1, sl 1, p1, k1, p1, k2tog, yo, k1, turn; (WS) yo, p3, (k1, p1) two times, k1, p7, (k1, p1) two times, k5.

Short row 11: (RS) K4, p1, sl 1, p2, k2tog, yo, k6, p1, sl 1, p2, k2tog, yo, k1, turn; (WS) yo, p3, k2, p1, k1, p8, k2, p1, k5.

Short row 12: (RS) K4, p1, sl 1, p1, k1, yo, ssk, (p1, k1) three times, p1, sl 1, p1, k3, turn; (WS) yo, p3, (k1, p1) four times, k1, p3, k1, p1, k5.

Short row 13: (RS) K4, p1, sl 1, p1, k2, yo, ssk, (p1, k1) two times, p2, sl 1, p1, k2, turn; (WS) yo, p2, k1, p1, k2, (p1, k1) two times, p4, k1, p1, k5.

Short row 14: (RS) K4, p1, sl 1, p1, k3, yo, ssk, (p1, k1) two times, p1, sl 1, p1, k1, turn; (WS) yo, (p1, k1) four times, p5, k1, p1, k5.

Short row 15: (RS) K4, p1, sl 1, p1, k4, yo, ssk, p1, k1, p2, sl 1, p1, turn; (WS) yo, k1, p1, k2, p1, k1, p6, k1, p1, k5.

Short row 16: (RS) K4, p1, sl 1, p1, k5, yo, ssk, (p1, k1) two times, turn; (WS) yo, (p1, k1) two times, p7, k1, p1, k5.

Short row 17: (RS) K4, p1, sl 1, p1, k6, yo, ssk, p2, turn; (WS) yo, k2, p8, k1, p1, k5.

Short row 18: (RS) K4, p1, sl 1, p1, (k1, p1) three times, k2tog, yo, k1, turn; (WS) yo, p3, (k1, p1) four times, k5.

Short row 19: (RS) K4, p1, sl 1, p2, (k1, p1) two times, k2tog, yo, k1, turn; (WS) yo, p3, (k1, p1) two times, k2, p1, k5.

Short row 20: (RS) K4, p1, sl 1, p1, (k1, p1) two times, k2tog, yo, k1, turn; (WS) yo, p3, (k1, p1) three times, k5.

Short row 21: (RS) K4, p1, sl 1, p2, k1, p1, k2tog, yo, k1, turn; (WS) yo, p3, k1, p1, k2, p1, k5.

Short row 22: (RS) K4, p1, sl 1, p1, k1, p1, k2tog, yo, k1, turn; (WS) yo, p3, (k1, p1) two times, k5.

Short row 23: (RS) K4, p1, sl 1, p2, k2tog, yo, k1, turn; (WS) yo, p3, k2, p1, k5.

Short row 24: (RS) K4, p1, sl 1, p1, k3, turn; (WS) yo, p3, k1, p1, k5.

Short row 25: (RS) K4, p1, sl 1, p1, k2, turn; (WS) yo, p2, k1, p1, k5.

Short row 26: (RS) K4, p1, sl 1, p1, k1, turn; (WS) yo, p1, k1, p1, k5.

Short row 27: (RS) K4, p1, sl 1, p1, turn; (WS) yo, k1, p1, k5.

Short row 28: (RS) K4, p1, k1, turn; (WS) yo, p1, k5.

Short row 29: (RS) K4, p1, turn; (WS) yo, k5.

Short row 30: (RS) K4, turn; (WS) yo, k4.

Short row 31: (RS) K3, turn; (WS) yo, k3.

Begin right corner edge

Right corner resolves short rows from left corner, one at a time, while building up short rows of its own. After the initial short row, there will be two yarnovers to resolve by decreasing with the stitch after gap.

See also right corner chart, page 135.

Short row 1: (RS) K3, k2tog (the yo and st after gap), turn; (WS) yo, k4.

Short row 2: (RS) K4, p3tog (the yo just made, the yo from left corner, and st after gap), turn; (WS) yo, k5.

Short row 3: (RS) K4, p1, k3tog (the yo just made, the yo from left corner, and st after gap), turn; (WS) yo, p1, k5.

Short row 4: (RS) K4, p1, sl 1, p3tog, turn; (WS) yo, k1, p1, k5.

Short row 5: (RS) K4, p1, sl 1, p1, p3tog, turn; (WS) yo, p1, k1, p1, k5.

Short row 6: (RS) K4, p1, sl 1, p1, k1, p3tog, turn; (WS) yo, p2, k1, p1, k5.

Short row 7: (RS) K4, p1, sl 1, p1, k2, p3tog, turn; (WS) yo, p3, k1, p1, k5.

Short row 8: (RS) K4, p1, sl 1, p1, k1, yo, ssk, p3tog, turn; (WS) yo, p4, k1, p1, k5.

Short row 9: (RS) K4, p1, sl 1, p1, k2, yo, ssk, p3tog, turn; (WS) yo, p5, k1, p1, k5.

Short row 10: (RS) K4, p1, sl 1, p1, k3, yo, ssk, p3tog, turn; (WS) yo, p6, k1, p1, k5.

Short row 11: (RS) K4, p1, sl 1, p1, k4, yo, ssk, p3tog, turn; (WS) yo, p7, k1, p1, k5.

Short row 12: (RS) K4, p1, sl 1, p1, k5, yo, ssk, p3tog, turn; (WS) yo, p8, k1, p1, k5.

Short row 13: (RS) K4, p1, sl 1, p1, k6, yo, ssk, p3tog, turn; (WS) yo, p9, k1, p1, k5.

Short row 14: (RS) K4, p1, sl 1, p1, (k1, p1) three times, k2tog, yo, k1, p3tog, turn; (WS) yo, k1, p3, (k1, p1) four times, k5.

Short row 15: (RS) K4, p1, sl 1, p2, (k1, p1) two times, k2tog, yo, k2, p1, k3tog, turn; (WS) yo, p1, k1, p4, (k1, p1) two times, k2, p1, k5.

Short row 16: (RS) K4, p1, sl 1, p1, (k1, p1) two times, k2tog, yo, k3, p1, sl 1, p3tog, turn; (WS) yo, k1, p1, k1, p5, (k1, p1) three times, k5.

Short row 17: (RS) K4, p1, sl 1, p2, k1, p1, k2tog, yo, k4, p1, sl 1, p1, p3tog, turn; (WS) yo, (p1, k1) two times, p6, k1, p1, k2, p1, k5.

Short row 18: (RS) K4, p1, sl 1, p1, k1, p1, k2tog, yo, k5, p1, sl 1, p1, k1, p3tog, turn; (WS) yo, p2, k1, p1, k1, p7, (k1, p1) two times, k5.

Short row 19: (RS) K4, p1, sl 1, p2, k2tog, yo, k6, p1, sl 1, p1, k2, p3tog, turn; (WS) yo, p3, k1, p1, k1, p8, k2, p1, k5.

Short row 20: (RS) K4, p1, sl 1, p1, k1, yo, ssk, (p1, k1) three times, p1, sl 1, p1, k1, yo, ssk, p3tog, turn; (WS) yo, p4, (k1, p1) four times, k1, p3, k1, p1, k5.

Short row 21: (RS) K4, p1, sl 1, p1, k2, yo, ssk, (p1, k1) two times, p2, sl 1, p1, k2, yo, ssk, p3tog, turn; (WS) yo, p5, k1, p1, k2, (p1, k1) two times, p4, k1, p1, k5.

Short row 22: (RS) K4, p1, sl 1, p1, k3, yo, ssk, (p1, k1) two times, p1, sl 1, p1, k3, yo, ssk, p3tog, turn; (WS) yo, p6, (k1, p1) three times, k1, p5, k1, p1, k5.

Short row 23: (RS) K4, p1, sl 1, p1, k4, yo, ssk, p1, k1, p2, sl 1, p1, k4, yo, ssk, p3tog, turn; (WS) yo, p7, k1, p1, k2, p1, k1, p6, k1, p1, k5.

Short row 24: (RS) K4, p1, sl 1, p1, k5, yo, ssk, p1, k1, p1, sl 1, p1, k5, yo, ssk, p3tog, turn; (WS) yo, p8, (k1, p1) two times, k1, p7, k1, p1, k5.

Short row 25: (RS) K4, p1, sl 1, p1, k6, yo, ssk, p2, sl 1, p1, k6, yo, ssk, p3tog, turn; (WS) yo, p9, k1, p1, k2, p8, k1, p1, k5.

Short row 26: (RS) K4, *p1, sl 1, p1, (k1, p1) three times, k2tog, yo, k1; rep from * one more time, p3tog, turn; (WS) yo, k1, *p3, (k1, p1) four times, k1; rep from * one more time, k4.

Short row 27: (RS) K4, *p1, sl 1, p2, (k1, p1) two times, k2tog, yo, k2; rep from * one more time, p1, k3tog, turn; (WS) yo, p1, k1, *p4, (k1, p1) two times, k2, p1, k1; rep from * one more time, k4.

Short row 28: (RS) K4, *p1, sl 1, p1, (k1, p1) two times, k2tog, yo, k3; rep from * one more time, p1, sl 1, p3tog, turn; (WS) yo, k1, p1, k1, *p5, (k1, p1) three times, k1; rep from * one more time, k4.

Short row 29: (RS) K4, *p1, sl 1, p2, k1, p1, k2tog, yo, k4; rep from * one more time, p1, sl 1, p1, k3tog, turn; (WS) yo, k2, p1, k1, *p6, k1, p1, k2, p1, k1; rep from * one more time, k4.

Short row 30: (RS) K4, *p1, sl 1, p1, k1, p1, k2tog, yo, k5; rep from * one more time, p1, sl 1, p1, k1, k3tog, turn; (WS) yo, k3, p1, k1, *p7, (k1, p1) two times, k1; rep from * one more time, k4.

Row 31: (RS) K4, *p1, sl 1, p2, k2tog, yo, k6; rep from * one more time, p1, sl 1, p1, k2, k3tog, k2 sts to end. *Place a locking st marker at the end of this RS row.*

Row 32: (WS) K6, p1, k1, *p8, k2, p1, k1; rep from * one more time, k4.

Continue right border

See Continue left border for row-by-row instructions.

See also main chart, next page.

Next row: (RS) Work Row 23 of main patt to end.

Next row: Work Row 24 of patt.

Work Rows 1-24 of main patt ten times.

Begin right border tip

See also right border tip chart, next page.

Note: Right border tip is worked the same as the left corner edge.

Work Short rows 1-31 of right border tip (see Begin left corner edge for row-by-row instructions).

Next row: (RS) K3, *k2tog (the yo with st after gap); rep from * to last 2 sts, k2. *Place a locking st marker at the end of this RS row.*

Next row: (WS) Bind off using the lacy bind off as follows: K1, *k1, return 2 sts to LH needle and k2tog-tbl; rep from * to end.

Begin pick up for body

With RS facing and beg at marker placed at right border, pick up and knit 122 sts to marker placed at center (1 st in each garter ridge), place marker for center, then pick up and knit 121 sts to marker placed at left border—243 sts on needle.

Next row *dec row:* (WS) Knit to marker (m), slip marker (sl m), k2tog, knit to end (1 st dec'd)—242 sts rem.

Begin shawl decreases

Next row *dec row:* (RS) K2, ssk, knit to 2 sts before m, k2tog, sl m, ssk, knit to last 4 sts, k2tog, k2 (4 sts dec'd)—238 sts rem.

Next row: Knit.

Rep the last 2 rows 57 more times—10 sts rem.

Next row *dec row:* (RS) K2, s2kp, remove m, s2kp, k2 (4 sts dec'd)—6 sts rem.

Next row: (WS) Bind off knitwise.

Finishing

Weave in ends. Wet block shawl to finished measurements.

Key

☐	knit on RS, purl on WS
●	purl on RS, knit on WS
V	sl 1 purlwise with yarn to WS
(	yo, p1 on WS (as for yo short row)
◉	yo, k1 on WS (as for yo short row)
O	yo
/	k2tog
\	ssk
✓•	p2tog on RS
⅄	dbl-dec [see Special abbreviations]
⅄	k3tog
⅄	p3tog on RS

Main pattern

Left border tip

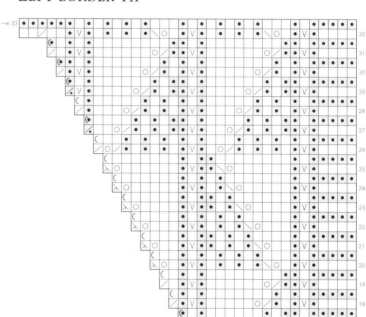

LEFT CORNER / RIGHT BORDER TIP

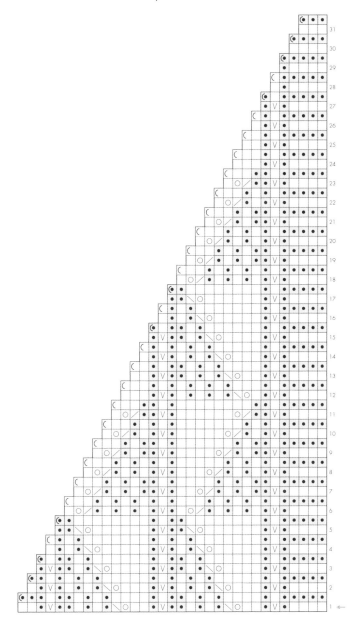

RIGHT CORNER

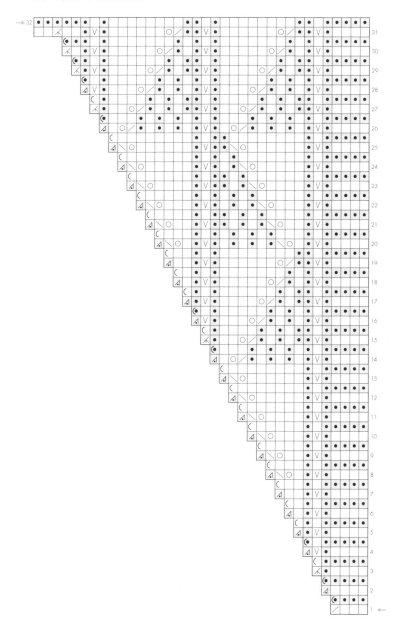

Hyssop

Finished measurements

76" [193 cm] wingspan and 30" [76 cm] deep at center

Yarn

Osprey by Quince & Co
(100% American wool; 170yd [155m]/100g)
- 5 skeins Storm 104

Needles

- One 32" circular needle in size US 9 [5.5 mm]

Or size to obtain gauge

Notions

- Stitch marker
- Tapestry needle

Gauge

12 sts and 20 rows = 4" [10 cm] in stitch pattern, after blocking.

Special abbreviations

make wrap: K5, *bring yarn to front, return these 5 stitches to LH needle, bring yarn to back, return these 5 stitches to RH needle; rep from * one more time.

Stitch pattern for swatching (mult of 12 sts + 7)

See also swatching chart, page 138.

Row 1: (RS) P4, *p3, make wrap, p4; rep from * to last 3 sts, p3.

Row 2 and all WS rows: Purl.

Row 3: K1, p3, *p2, k2tog, k1, (yo, k1) two times, ssk, p3; rep from * to last 3 sts, p2, k1.

Row 5: K2, p2, *p1, k2tog, k1, yo, k3, yo, k1, ssk, p2; rep from * to last 3 sts, p1, k2.

Row 7: K3, p1, *k2tog, k1, yo, k2tog, yo, k1, yo, ssk, yo, k1, ssk, p1; rep from * to last 3 sts, k3.

Row 9: K1, make wrap, *p7, make wrap; rep from * to last st, k1.

Row 11: K4, *yo, k1, ssk, p5, k2tog, k1, yo, k1; rep from * to last 3 sts, k3.

Row 13: K4, *k1, yo, k1, ssk, p3, k2tog, k1, yo, k2; rep from * to last 3 sts, k3.

Row 15: K4, *yo, ssk, yo, k1, ssk, p1, k2tog, k1, yo, k2tog, yo, k1; rep from * to last 3 sts, k3.

Row 16: (WS) Purl.

Repeat Rows 1-16 for stitch pattern for swatching.

Note

Hyssop's body is knitted flat from the bottom up, increasing at each side edge to wide top edge, then stitches are picked up along side edges and border is worked in garter stitch.

SHAWL

Using the long-tail cast on, CO 5 sts.

Begin shawl set up

See also set up chart, next page.

Row 1 *inc row:* (RS) K1, yo, k3, yo, k1 (2 sts inc'd)—7 sts.

Row 2: Purl.

Row 3: K1, make wrap, k1.

Row 4 *inc row:* P1, yo, p5, yo, p1—9 sts.

Row 5 *inc row:* K1, yo, k2tog, (k1, yo) two times, k1, ssk, yo, k1—11 sts.

Row 6 *inc row:* P1, yo, p9, yo, p1—13 sts.

Row 7 *inc row:* K1, yo, k1, k2tog, k1, yo, k3, yo, k1, ssk, k1, yo, k1—15 sts.

Row 8 *inc row:* P1, yo, p13, yo, p1—17 sts.

Row 9 *inc row:* K1, yo, k2, k2tog, k1, yo, k2tog, yo, k1, yo, ssk, yo, k1, ssk, k2, yo, k1—19 sts.

Row 10: Purl.

Begin shawl increases

See also main chart, next page.

Row 1: (RS) K1, *make wrap, p7; rep from * to last 6 sts, make wrap, k1.

Row 2 *inc row:* P1, yo, purl to last st, yo, p1 (2 sts inc'd)—21 sts.

Row 3 *inc row:* K1, yo, k2tog, k1, yo, *k1, yo, k1, ssk, p5, k2tog, k1, yo; rep from * to last 5 sts, k1, yo, k1, ssk, yo, k1 (2 sts inc'd)—23 sts.

Row 4 *inc row:* P1, yo, purl to last st, yo, p1—25 sts.

Row 5 *inc row:* K1, yo, k1, k2tog, k1, yo, k1, *k2, yo, k1, ssk, p3, k2tog, k1, yo, k1; rep from * to last 7 sts, k2, yo, k1, ssk, k1, yo, k1—27 sts.

Row 6 *inc row:* P1, yo, purl to last st, yo, p1—29 sts.

Row 7 *inc row:* K1, yo, k2, k2tog, k1, yo, k2tog, yo, *k1, yo, ssk, yo, k1, ssk, p1, k2tog, k1, yo, k2tog, yo; rep from * to last 9 sts, k1, yo, ssk, yo, k1, ssk, k2, yo, k1—31 sts.

Row 8: Purl.

Rep the last 8 rows 14 more times—199 sts.

Next row: (RS) K1, *make wrap, k7; rep from * to last 6 sts, make wrap, k1.

Next row: Knit.

Begin top trim

Next row *inc row:* (RS) K1, yo, knit to last st, yo, k1 (2 sts inc'd)—201 sts.

Next row: Knit to end, knitting yarnovers through the back loop.

Rep the last 2 rows one more time, then work *inc row* one more time—205 sts.

Next row: (WS) Bind off using the lacy bind off as follows: K1, *k1, return 2 sts to LH needle and k2tog-tbl; rep from * to end.

Gently steam block piece.

Begin border pick up

With RS facing and beg at left tip of shawl body, pick up and knit 102 sts along left side edge (1 st in each garter ridge along top trim and 1 st in each yo), pick up and knit 1 st in CO st beside the final yo, place marker for center, pick up and knit 1 st in each of next 2 CO sts, then pick up and knit 102 sts along right side edge to end—207 sts on needle.

First row: (WS) Knit.

Begin border increases

Next row *inc row:* (RS) K1-f/b, knit to 1 st before marker, k1-f/b, slip marker, k1-f/b, knit to last st, k1-f/b (4 sts inc'd)—211 sts.

Next row: Knit.

Rep the last 2 rows five more times, then work *inc row* one more time—235 sts.

Next row: (WS) Bind off using the lacy bind off as follows: K1, *k1, return 2 sts to LH needle and k2tog-tbl; rep from * to end.

Finishing

Weave in ends. Wet block shawl to finished measurements.

Key

☐ knit on RS, purl on WS

● purl on RS

⊙ yo

⊘ k2tog

⊠ ssk

▭ make wrap [see Special abbreviations]

☐ pattern repeat

Main pattern

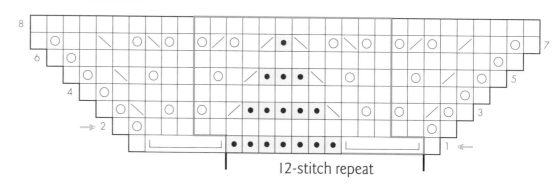

12-stitch repeat

Swatching pattern

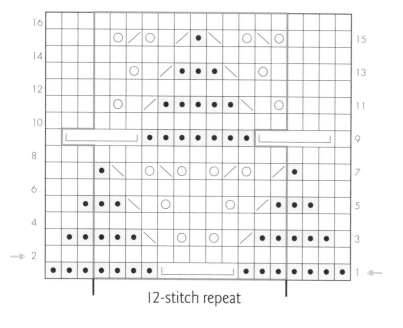

12-stitch repeat

Pattern set up

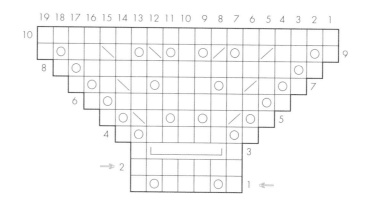

138

Finished measurements
80" [203 cm] wingspan and 27" [68.5 cm] deep at center

Yarn
Lark by Quince & Co
(100% American wool; 134yd [123m]/50g)
• 7 skeins Audouin 157

Needles
• One 24" circular needle in size US 8 [5 mm]
Or size to obtain gauge

Notions
• Tapestry needle

Gauge
19 sts and 24 rows = 4" [10 cm] in stitch pattern, after blocking.

Special abbreviations
sl 1: Slip 1 stitch purlwise with yarn in back.

Stitch pattern for swatching (mult of 12 sts)
See also swatching chart, page 144.
Row 1: (RS) *K1, yo, ssk, (p1, k1) three times, p1, sl 1, p1; rep from * to end.
Row 2: *K1, (p1, k1) four times, p3; rep from *.
Row 3: *K2, yo, ssk, (p1, k1) two times, p2, sl 1, p1; rep from *.
Row 4: *K1, p1, k2, (p1, k1) two times, p4; rep from *.
Row 5: *K3, yo, ssk, (p1, k1) two times, p1, sl 1, p1; rep from *.
Row 6: *K1, (p1, k1) three times, p5; rep from *.
Row 7: *K4, yo, ssk, p1, k1, p2, sl 1, p1; rep from *.

Row 8: *K1, p1, k2, p1, k1, p6; rep from *.
Row 9: *K5, yo, ssk, p1, k1, p1, sl 1, p1; rep from *.
Row 10: *K1, (p1, k1) two times, p7; rep from *.
Row 11: *K6, yo, ssk, p2, sl 1, p1; rep from *.
Row 12: *K1, p1, k2, p8; rep from *.
Row 13: *(K1, p1) three times, k2tog, yo, k1, p1, sl 1, p1; rep from *.
Row 14: *K1, p1, k1, p3, (k1, p1) three times; rep from *.
Row 15: *P1, (k1, p1) two times, k2tog, yo, k2, p1, sl 1, p1; rep from *.
Row 16: *K1, p1, k1, p4, k1, (p1, k1) two times; rep from *.
Row 17: *(K1, p1) two times, k2tog, yo, k3, p1, sl 1, p1; rep from *.
Row 18: *K1, p1, k1, p5, (k1, p1) two times; rep from *.
Row 19: *P1, k1, p1, k2tog, yo, k4, p1, sl 1, p1; rep from *.
Row 20: *K1, p1, k1, p6, k1, p1, k1; rep from *.
Row 21: *K1, p1, k2tog, yo, k5, p1, sl 1, p1; rep from *.
Row 22: *K1, p1, k1, p7, k1, p1; rep from *.
Row 23: *P1, k2tog, yo, k6, p1, sl 1, p1; rep from *.
Row 24: *K1, p1, k1, p8, k1; rep from *.
Repeat Rows 1-24 for stitch pattern for swatching.

Note
Reishi is knitted flat from side to side, beginning at left tip, increasing to widest point at center, then decreasing to right tip.

REISHI

SHAWL

Using the long-tail cast on, CO 3 sts.
First row: (WS) K1, p1, k1.

Begin shawl set up

See also set up chart, page 144.

Row 1: (RS) P1, (k1, p1, k1) in next st, p1 (2 sts inc'd)—5 sts.
Row 2: K1, (p1, k1) two times.
Row 3: P1, (sl 1, p1) two times.
Row 4: K1, (p1, k1) two times.
Row 5: P1, (k1, p1, k1) in next st, p1, sl 1, p1 (2 sts inc'd)—7 sts.
Row 6: K1, (p1, k1) three times.
Row 7: P1, (sl 1, p1) three times
Row 8: K1, (p1, k1) three times.
Row 9: P1, sl 1, p1, m1-p/L, (sl 1, p1) two times (1 st inc'd)—8 sts.
Row 10: (K1, p1) two times, k2, p1, k1.
Row 11: P1, sl 1, k1, M1R, p1, (sl 1, p1) two times—9 sts.
Row 12: K1, (p1, k1) four times.
Row 13: P1, sl 1, p1, M1R, k1, p1, (sl 1, p1) two times—10 sts.
Row 14: K1, (p1, k1) two times, p2, k1, p1, k1.
Row 15: P1, sl 1, p1, k1, yo, k1, p1, (sl 1, p1) two times—11 sts.
Row 16: K1, (p1, k1) two times, p3, k1, p1, k1.
Row 17: P1, sl 1, p1, k1, yo, knit to last 5 sts, p1, (sl 1, p1) two times—12 sts.
Row 18: K1, (p1, k1) two times, purl to last 3 sts, k1, p1, k1.
Rows 19-26: Rep Rows 17 and 18 four times—16 sts.
Row 27: (RS) P1, sl 1, p1, M1R, yo, ssk, p1, (k1, p1) three times, (sl 1, p1) two times—17 sts.
Row 28: K1, (p1, k1) five times, p3, k1, p1, k1.

Begin shawl increases

See also increase chart, page 144.

Row 1: (RS) P1, sl 1, p1, m1-p/L, *k2, yo, ssk, (p1, k1) two times, p2, sl 1, p1; rep from * to last 2 sts, sl 1, p1 (1 st inc'd)—18 sts.
Row 2: K1, p1, *k1, p1, k2, (p1, k1) two times, p4; rep from * to last 4 sts, k2, p1, k1.
Row 3: P1, sl 1, p1, M1R, p1, *k3, yo, ssk, p1, (k1, p1) two times, sl 1, p1; rep from * to last 2 sts, sl 1, p1—19 sts.
Row 4: K1, p1, *k1, (p1, k1) three times, p5; rep from * to last 5 sts, k1, (p1, k1) two times.
Row 5: P1, sl 1, p1, m1-p/L, sl 1, p1, *k4, yo, ssk, p1, k1, p2, sl 1, p1; rep from * to last 2 sts, sl 1, p1—20 sts.
Row 6: K1, p1, *k1, p1, k2, p1, k1, p6; rep from * to last 6 sts, k1, p1, k2, p1, k1.
Row 7: P1, sl 1, p1, M1R, p1, sl 1, p1, *k5, yo, ssk, p1, k1, p1, sl 1, p1; rep from * to last 2 sts, sl 1, p1—21 sts.
Row 8: K1, p1, *k1, (p1, k1) two times, p7; rep from * to last 7 sts, k1, (p1, k1) three times.
Row 9: P1, sl 1, p1, M1R, k1, p1, sl 1, p1, *k6, yo, ssk, p2, sl 1, p1; rep from * to last 2 sts, sl 1, p1—22 sts.
Row 10: K1, p1, *k1, p1, k2, p8; rep from * to last 8 sts, k1, p1, k1, p2, k1, p1, k1.
Row 11: P1, sl 1, p1, k1, yo, k1, p1, sl 1, p1, *(k1, p1) three times, k2tog, yo, k1, p1, sl 1, p1; rep from * to last 2 sts, sl 1, p1—23 sts.
Row 12: K1, p1, *k1, p1, k1, p3, (k1, p1) three times; rep from * to last 9 sts, k1, p1, k1, p3, k1, p1, k1.
Row 13: P1, sl 1, p1, k1, yo, k2, p1, sl 1, p1, *p1, (k1, p1) two times, k2tog, yo, k2, p1, sl 1, p1; rep from * to last 2 sts, sl 1, p1—24 sts.

Row 14: K1, p1, *k1, p1, k1, p4, k1, (p1, k1) two times; rep from * to last 10 sts, k1, p1, k1, p4, k1, p1, k1.
Row 15: P1, sl 1, p1, k1, yo, k3, p1, sl 1, p1, *(k1, p1) two times, k2tog, yo, k3, p1, sl 1, p1; rep from * to last 2 sts, sl 1, p1—25 sts.
Row 16: K1, p1, *k1, p1, k1, p5, (k1, p1) two times; rep from * to last 11 sts, k1, p1, k1, p5, k1, p1, k1.
Row 17: P1, sl 1, p1, k1, yo, k4, p1, sl 1, p1, *p1, k1, p1, k2tog, yo, k4, p1, sl 1, p1; rep from * to last 2 sts, sl 1, p1—26 sts.
Row 18: K1, p1, *k1, p1, k1, p6, k1, p1, k1; rep from * to end.
Row 19: P1, sl 1, p1, k1, yo, k5, p1, sl 1, p1, *k1, p1, k2tog, yo, k5, p1, sl 1, p1; rep from * to last 2 sts, sl 1, p1—27 sts.
Row 20: K1, p1, *k1, p1, k1, p7, k1, p1; rep from * to last st, k1.
Row 21: P1, sl 1, p1, k1, yo, k6, p1, sl 1, p1, *p1, k2tog, yo, k6, p1, sl 1, p1; rep from * to last 2 sts, sl 1, p1—28 sts.
Row 22: K1, p1, *k1, p1, k1, p8, k1; rep from * to last 2 sts, p1, k1.
Row 23: P1, sl 1, p1, M1R, yo, ssk, (p1, k1) three times, p1, sl 1, p1, *k1, yo, ssk, (p1, k1) three times, p1, sl 1, p1; rep from * to last 2 sts, sl 1, p1—29 sts.
Row 24: K1, p1, *k1, (p1, k1) four times, p3; rep from * to last 3 sts, k1, p1, k1.
Rep Rows 1-24 eight more times—125 sts on needle.

Begin shawl decreases

See also decrease chart, page 145.

Row 1: (RS) P1, sl 1, p1, k2tog, yo, ssk, (p1, k1) two times, p2, sl 1, p1, *k2, yo, ssk, (p1, k1) two times, p2, sl 1, p1; rep from * to last 2 sts, sl 1, p1 (1 st dec'd)—124 sts rem.

Row 2: K1, p1, *k1, p1, k2, (p1, k1) two times, p4; rep from * to last 14 sts, k1, p1, k2, (p1, k1) two times, p3, k1, p1, k1.

Row 3: P1, sl 1, p1, k2tog, yo, ssk, p1, (k1, p1) two times, sl 1, p1, *k3, yo, ssk, p1, (k1, p1) two times, sl 1, p1; rep from * to last 2 sts, sl 1, p1—123 sts rem.

Row 4: K1, p1, *k1, (p1, k1) three times, p5; rep from * to last 13 sts, k1, (p1, k1) three times, p3, k1, p1, k1.

Row 5: P1, sl 1, p1, k2tog, yo, ssk, p1, k1, p2, sl 1, p1, *k4, yo, ssk, p1, k1, p2, sl 1, p1; rep from * to last 2 sts, sl 1, p1—122 sts rem.

Row 6: K1, p1, *k1, p1, k2, p1, k1, p6; rep from * to last 12 sts, k1, p1, k2, p1, k1, p3, k1, p1, k1.

Row 7: P1, sl 1, p1, k2tog, yo, ssk, p1, k1, p1, sl 1, p1, *k5, yo, ssk, p1, k1, p1, sl 1, p1; rep from * to last 2 sts, sl 1, p1—121 sts rem.

Row 8: K1, p1, *k1, (p1, k1) two times, p7; rep from * to last 11 sts, k1, (p1, k1) two times, p3, k1, p1, k1.

Row 9: P1, sl 1, p1, k2tog, yo, ssk, p2, sl 1, p1, *k6, yo, ssk, p2, sl 1, p1; rep from * to last 2 sts, sl 1, p1—120 sts rem.

Row 10: K1, p1, *k1, p1, k2, p8; rep from * to last 10 sts, k1, p1, k2, p3, k1, p1, k1.

Row 11: P1, sl 1, p1, k3tog, yo, k1, p1, sl 1, p1, *(k1, p1) three times, k2tog, yo, k1, p1, sl 1, p1; rep from * to last 2 sts, sl 1, p1—119 sts rem.

Row 12: K1, p1, *k1, p1, k1, p3, (k1, p1) three times; rep from * to last 9 sts, k1, p1, k1, p3, k1, p1, k1.

Row 13: P1, sl 1, p1, k2tog, k1, p1, sl 1, p1, *p1, (k1, p1) two times, k2tog, yo, k2, p1, sl 1, p1; rep from * to last 2 sts, sl 1, p1—118 sts rem.

Row 14: K1, p1, *k1, p1, k1, p4, k1, (p1, k1) two times; rep from * to last 8 sts, k1, p1, k1, p2, k1, p1, k1.

Row 15: P1, sl 1, p1, k2tog, p1, sl 1, p1, *(k1, p1) two times, k2tog, yo, k3, p1, sl 1, p1; rep from * to last 2 sts, sl 1, p1—117 sts rem.

Row 16: K1, p1, *k1, p1, k1, p5, (k1, p1) two times; rep from * to last 7 sts, k1, (p1, k1) three times.

Row 17: P1, sl 1, p1, k2tog, sl 1, p1, *p1, k1, p1, k2tog, yo, k4, p1, sl 1, p1; rep from * to last 2 sts, sl 1, p1—116 sts rem.

Row 18: K1, p1, *k1, p1, k1, p6, k1, p1, k1; rep from * to last 6 sts, k1, p2, k1, p1, k1.

Row 19: P1, sl 1, p1, k2tog, p1, *k1, p1, k2tog, yo, k5, p1, sl 1, p1; rep from * to last 2 sts, sl 1, p1—115 sts rem.

Row 20: K1, p1, *k1, p1, k1, p7, k1, p1; rep from * to last 5 sts, k1, (p1, k1) two times.

Row 21: P1, sl 1, p1, k2tog, *p1, k2tog, yo, k6, p1, sl 1, p1; rep from * to last 2 sts, sl 1, p1—114 sts rem.

Row 22: K1, p1, *k1, p1, k1, p8, k1; rep from * to last 4 sts, (p1, k1) two times.

Row 23: P1, sl 1, p1, k2tog, yo, ssk, (p1, k1) three times, p1, sl 1, p1, *k1, yo, ssk, (p1, k1) three times, p1, sl 1, p1; rep from * to last 2 sts, sl 1, p1—113 sts rem.

Row 24: K1, p1, *k1, (p1, k1) four times, p3; rep from * to last 3 sts, k1, p1, k1.

Rep Rows 1-24 seven more times—29 sts rem.

End shawl decreases

See also end chart, page 145.

Row 1: (RS) P1, sl 1, p1, k2tog, yo, ssk, (p1, k1) two times, p2, sl 1, p1, k2, yo, ssk, (p1, k1) two times, p2, (sl 1, p1) two times (1 st dec'd)—28 sts rem.

Row 2: (K1, p1) two times, k2, (p1, k1) two times, p4, k1, p1, k2, (p1, k1) two times, p3, k1, p1, k1.

Row 3: P1, sl 1, p1, k2tog, yo, ssk, p1, (k1, p1) two times, sl 1, p1, k3, yo, ssk, p1, (k1, p1) two times, (sl 1, p1) two times—27 sts rem.

Row 4: K1, (p1, k1) four times, p5, k1, (p1, k1) three times, p3, k1, p1, k1.

Row 5: P1, sl 1, p1, k2tog, yo, ssk, p1, k1, p2, sl 1, p1, k4, yo, ssk, p1, k1, p2, (sl 1, p1) two times—26 sts rem.

Row 6: (K1, p1) two times, k2, p1, k1, p6, k1, p1, k2, p1, k1, p3, k1, p1, k1.

Row 7: P1, sl 1, p1, k2tog, yo, ssk, p1, k1, p1, sl 1, p1, k5, yo, ssk, p1, k1, p1, (sl 1, p1) two times—25 sts rem.

Row 8: K1, (p1, k1) three times, p7, k1, (p1, k1) two times, p3, k1, p1, k1.

Row 9: P1, sl 1, p1, k2tog, yo, ssk, p2, sl 1, p1, k6, yo, ssk, p2, (sl 1, p1) two times—24 sts rem.

Row 10: (K1, p1) two times, k2, p8, k1, p1, k2, p3, k1, p1, k1.

Row 11: P1, sl 1, p1, k3tog, yo, k1, p1, sl 1, p1, (k1, p1) three times, k2tog, yo, k1, p1, (sl 1, p1) two times—23 sts rem.

Row 12: K1, (p1, k1) two times, p3, (k1, p1) four times, k1, p3, k1, p1, k1.

Row 13: P1, sl 1, p1, k2tog, k1, p1, sl 1, p2, (k1, p1) two times, k2tog, yo, k2, p1, (sl 1, p1) two times—22 sts rem.

Row 14: K1, (p1, k1) two times, p4, (k1, p1) two times, k2, p1, k1, p2, k1, p1, k1.

Row 15: P1, sl 1, p1, k2tog, p1, sl 1, p1, (k1, p1) two times, k2tog, yo, k3, p1, (sl 1, p1) two times—21 sts rem.
Row 16: K1, (p1, k1) two times, p5, (k1, p1) five times, k1.
Row 17: P1, sl 1, p1, k2tog, sl 1, p2, k1, p1, k2tog, yo, k4, p1, (sl 1, p1) two times—20 sts rem.
Row 18: K1, (p1, k1) two times, p6, k1, p1, k2, p2, k1, p1, k1.
Row 19: P1, sl 1, p1, k2tog, p1, k1, p1, k2tog, yo, k5, p1, (sl 1, p1) two times—19 sts rem.
Row 20: K1, (p1, k1) two times, p7, k1, (p1, k1) three times.
Row 21: P1, sl 1, p1, k2tog, p1, k2tog, yo, k6, p1, (sl 1, p1) two times—18 sts rem.
Row 22: K1, (p1, k1) two times, p8, k1, (p1, k1) two times.
Row 23: P1, sl 1, p1, k2tog, yo, ssk, (p1, k1) three times, p1, (sl 1, p1) two times—17 sts rem.
Row 24: K1, (p1, k1) five times, p3, k1, p1, k1.
Row 25: P1, sl 1, p1, k2tog, yo, ssk, (p1, k1) two times, p2, (sl 1, p1) two times—16 sts rem.
Row 26: (K1, p1) two times, k2, (p1, k1) two times, p3, k1, p1, k1.
Row 27: P1, sl 1, p1, k2tog, yo, ssk, p1, (k1, p1) two times, (sl 1, p1) two times—15 sts rem.
Row 28: K1, (p1, k1) four times, p3, k1, p1, k1.
Row 29: P1, sl 1, p1, k2tog, yo, ssk, p1, k1, p2, (sl 1, p1) two times—14 sts rem.
Row 30: (K1, p1) two times, k2, p1, k1, p3, k1, p1, k1.
Row 31: P1, sl 1, p1, k2tog, yo, ssk, p1, k1, p1, (sl 1, p1) two times—13 sts rem.
Row 32: K1, (p1, k1) three times, p3, k1, p1, k1.
Row 33: P1, sl 1, p1, k2tog, yo, ssk, p2, (sl 1, p1) two times—12 sts rem.
Row 34: (K1, p1) two times, k2, p3, k1, p1, k1.

Row 35: P1, sl 1, p1, k3tog, yo, k1, p1, (sl 1, p1) two times—11 sts rem.
Row 36: K1, (p1, k1) two times, p3, k1, p1, k1.
Row 37: P1, sl 1, p1, k2tog, k1, p1, (sl 1, p1) two times—10 sts rem.
Row 38: K1, (p1, k1) two times, p2, k1, p1, k1.
Row 39: P1, sl 1, p1, k2tog, p1, (sl 1, p1) two times—9 sts rem.
Row 40: K1, (p1, k1) four times.
Row 41: P1, sl 1, p1, p2tog, (sl 1, p1) two times—8 sts rem.
Row 42: (K1, p1) two times, k2, p1, k1.
Row 43: P1, sl 1, p2tog, (sl 1, p1) two times—7 sts rem.

Row 44: K1, (p1, k1) three times.
Row 45: P1, sssk, p1, sl 1, p1 (2 sts dec'd)—5 sts rem.
Row 46: K1, (p1, k1) two times.
Row 47: P1, (sl 1, p1) two times.
Row 48: K1, (p1, k1) two times.
Row 49: P1, sssk, p1 (2 sts dec'd)—3 sts rem.
Next row: (WS) Bind off purlwise.

Finishing
Weave in ends. Wet block shawl to finished measurements.

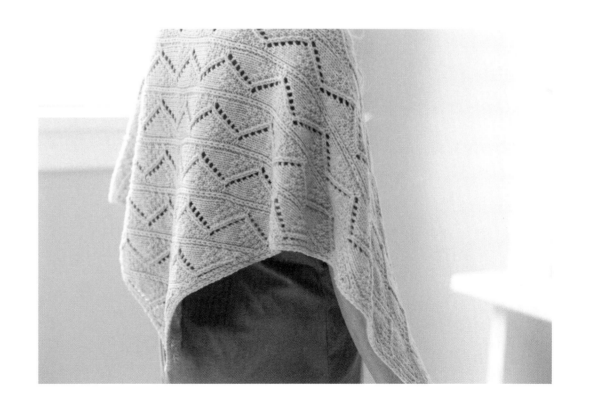

Shawl set up

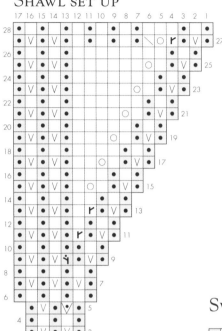

Key

☐	knit on RS, purl on WS	◢	p2tog
▪	purl on RS, knit on WS	V	sl 1 purlwise with yarn in back
O	yo	ꞁ	M1R
◿	k2tog	ꞁ	m1-p/L on RS
◺	ssk	V̇	(k1, p1, k1) in st
◿	k3tog	☐	pattern repeat
◺	sssk	│	marker placement

Swatching pattern

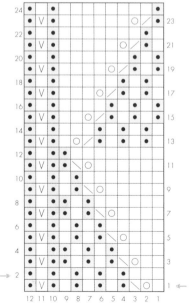

Increase pattern

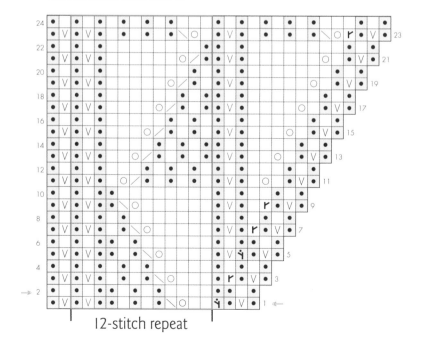

12-stitch repeat

PATTERN END

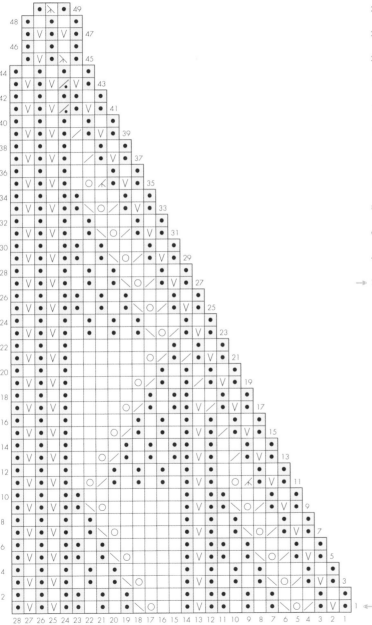

DECREASE PATTERN

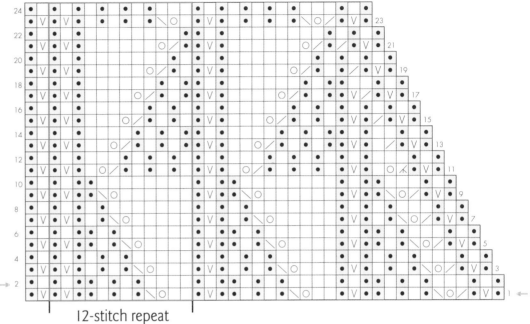

12-stitch repeat

CHAGA

Finished measurements

60 (88)" [152.5 (223.5) cm] wingspan and 35 (42)" [89 (106.5) cm] at deepest point; shown in larger size

Yarn

Crane by Quince & Co

(50% super kid mohair, 50% superfine merino; 208yd [146m]/~100g)

- 3 (7) skeins Quanah 619

Needles

- One 32" circular needle in size US 8 [5 mm]

Or size to obtain gauge

Notions

- Stitch markers
- Cable needle (optional)
- Tapestry needle

Gauge

16 sts and 24 rows = 4" [10 cm] in stockinette stitch, after blocking.

Special abbreviations

sl: Slip specified number of stitches purlwise with yarn held to the WS of work (unless otherwise specified).

CIL (cross 1 over 2 left): Slip 1 stitch onto cable needle (cn) and hold in front, k2, then k1 from cn.

CIR (cross 1 over 2 right): Slip 2 stitches onto cn and hold in back, k1, then k2 from cn.

Notes

1. Chaga is knitted flat, from side to side, beginning at wide left edge and decreasing to right tip.
2. Stitch count varies from row to row in lace pattern. Once shawl shaping begins, stitch counts are provided periodically in each section to help keep track.
3. All slipped stitches are slipped purlwise except the first stitch of every RS row, this stitch is slipped knitwise.

SHAWL

Using the long-tail cast on, CO 155 (239) sts. Do not join.

First row: (WS) Purl.

Begin lace border

See also border chart, page 150.

Note: First stitch of every RS row throughout pattern is slipped knitwise with yarn in back. All other slipped stitches are slipped purlwise with yarn held to the WS.

Row 1: (RS) Sl 1, *k2, sl 2, k2, yo, k1, ssk, p1, k2tog, k1, p1, k1, ssk, p1, k2tog, k1, yo; rep from * to last 7 sts, k2, sl 2, k2, sl 1 (2 sts dec'd each repeat)—141 (217) sts.

Row 2: P3, sl 2, p2, *p3, (k1, p2) two times, k1, p5, sl 2, p2; rep from * to last st, p1.

Row 3: Sl 1, *CIR, CIL, yo, k1, yo, ssk, p1, k2tog, p1, ssk, p1, k2tog, yo, k1, yo; rep from * to last 7 sts, CIR, CIL, sl 1.

Row 4: P7, *p4, (k1, p1) two times, k1, p10; rep from * to last st, p1.

Row 5: Sl 1, *k2, sl 2, k2, yo, k3, yo, sk2p, p1, k3tog, yo, k3, yo; rep from * to last 7 sts, k2, sl 2, k2, sl 1.

Row 6: P3, sl 2, p2, *p6, k1, p8, sl 2, p2; rep from * to last st, p1.

Row 7: Sl 1, *CIR, CIL, yo, k5, yo, sk2p, yo, k5, yo; rep from * to last 7 sts, CIR, CIL, sl 1 (2 sts inc'd each repeat)—155 (239) sts.

Row 8: Purl.

Row 9: Sl 1, *k2, sl 2, k2, yo, k1, ssk, p1, k2tog, (k1, yo) two times, k1, ssk, p1, k2tog, k1, yo; rep from * to last 7 sts, k2, sl 2, k2, sl 1.

Row 10: P3, sl 2, p2, *p3, k1, p7, k1, p5, sl 2, p2; rep from * to last st, p1.

Row 11: Sl 1, *CIR, CIL, yo, k1, ssk, p1, k2tog, k1, p1, k1, ssk, p1, k2tog, k1, yo; rep from * to last 7 sts, CIR, CIL, sl 1 (2 sts dec'd each repeat)—141 (217) sts.

Row 12: P7, *p3, (k1, p2) two times, k1, p9; rep from * to last st, p1.

Row 13: Sl 1, *k2, sl 2, k2, yo, k1, yo, ssk, p1, k2tog, p1, ssk, p1, k2tog, yo, k1, yo; rep from * to last 7 sts, k2, sl 2, k2, sl 1.

Row 14: P3, sl 2, p2, *p4, (k1, p1) two times, k1, p6, sl 2, p2; rep from * to last st, p1.

Row 15: Sl 1, *C1R, C1L, yo, k3, yo, sk2p, p1, k3tog, yo, k3, yo; rep from * to last 7 sts, C1R, C1L, sl 1.

Row 16: P7, *p6, k1, p12; rep from * to last st, p1.

Row 17: Sl 1, *k2, sl 2, k2, yo, k5, yo, sk2p, yo, k5, yo; rep from * to last 7 sts, k2, sl 2, k2, sl 1 (2 sts inc'd each repeat)—155 (239) sts.

Row 18: P3, sl 2, p2, *p17, sl 2, p2; rep from * to last st, p1.

Row 19: Sl 1, *C1R, C1L, yo, k1, ssk, p1, k2tog, (k1, yo) two times, k1, ssk, p1, k2tog, k1, yo; rep from * to last 7 sts, C1R, C1L, sl 1.

Row 20: P7, *p3, k1, p7, k1, p9; rep from * to last st, p1.

Row 21: Sl 1, *k2, sl 2, k2, yo, k1, ssk, p1, k2tog, k1, p1, k1, ssk, p1, k2tog, k1, yo; rep from * to last 7 sts, k2, sl 2, k2, sl 1 (2 sts dec'd each repeat)—141 (217) sts.

Row 22 *place marker:* P3, sl 2, p5, (k1, p2) two times, k1, p5, sl 2, p2, place marker for pattern (pm), *p3, (k1, p2) two times, k1, p5, sl 2, p2; rep from * to last st, p1.

Begin decrease set up

See also set up chart, page 151.

Row 1: (RS) Sl 1, *C1R, C1L, yo, k1, yo, ssk, p1, k2tog, p1, ssk, p1, k2tog, yo, k1, yo; rep from * to marker (m), C1R, C1L, yo, k1, yo, ssk, p1, k2tog, p1, ssk, p1, k2tog, yo, k1, C1R, C1L, sl 1 (1 st dec'd)—140 (216) sts.

Row 2 *place marker:* P10, (k1, p1) two times, k1, p3, p1-tbl, p6, slip marker (sl m), *p1-tbl, p3, (k1, p1) two times, k1, p3, p1-tbl, p6; rep from * to last 20 sts, pm for border, p4, (k1, p1) two times, k1, p11.

Row 3: Sl 1, k2, sl 2, k2, yo, k3, yo, sk2p, p1, k3tog, yo, k3, yo, sl m, *k2, sl 2, k2, yo, k3, yo, sk2p, p1, k3tog, yo, k3, yo; rep from * to next m, k2, sl 2, k2, yo, k3, yo, sk2p, p1, k3tog, yo, k4, sl 2, k2, sl 1 (1 st dec'd)—139 (215) sts.

Row 4: P3, sl 2, p6, k1, p5, p1-tbl, p2, sl 2, p2, sl m, *p1-tbl, p5, k1, p5, p1-tbl, p2, sl 2, p2; rep from * to next m, p6, k1, p8, sl 2, p3.

Row 5: Sl 1, C1R, C1L, yo, k5, yo, sk2p, yo, k5, yo, sl m, *C1R, C1L, yo, k5, yo, sk2p, yo, k5, yo; rep from * to next m, C1R, C1L, yo, k5, yo, sk2p, yo, k3, C1R, C1L, sl 1 (2 sts inc'd each rep and 1 st dec'd)—152 (236) sts.

Row 6: P18, p1-tbl, p6, sl m, *p1-tbl, p13, p1-tbl, p6; rep from * to next m, purl to end.

Row 7: Sl 1, k2, sl 2, k2, yo, k1, ssk, p1, k2tog, (k1, yo) two times, k1, ssk, p1, k2tog, k1, yo, sl m, *k2, sl 2, k17; rep from * to next m, k2, sl 2, k16, sl 2, k2, sl 1.

Row 8: P3, sl 2, p16, sl 2, p2, sl m, *p17, sl 2, p2; rep from * to next m, p3, k1, p7, k1, p5, sl 2, p3.

Row 9: Sl 1, C1R, C1L, yo, k1, ssk, p1, k2tog, k1, p1, k1, ssk, p1, k2tog, k1, yo, sl m, *C1R, C1L, k15; rep from * to next m, C1R, C1L, k10, ssk, C1R, C1L, sl 1 (1 st dec'd).

Row 10: Purl to last m, p3, (k1, p2) two times, k1, p10.

Row 11: Sl 1, k2, sl 2, k2, yo, k1, yo, ssk, p1, k2tog, p1, ssk, p1, k2tog, yo, k1, yo, sl m, *k2, sl 2, k17; rep from * to next m, k2, sl 2, k11, ssk, k2, sl 2, k2, sl 1 (1 st dec'd).

Row 12: P3, sl 2, p14, sl 2, p2, sl m, *p17, sl 2, p2; rep from * to next m, p4, (k1, p1) two times, k1, p6, sl 2, p3.

Row 13: Sl 1, C1R, C1L, yo, k3, yo, sk2p, p1, k3tog, yo, k3, yo, sl m, *C1R, C1L, k15; rep from * to next m, C1R, C1L, k8, ssk, C1R, C1L, sl 1 (1 st dec'd).

Row 14: Purl to last m, p6, k1, p13.

Row 15: Sl 1, k2, sl 2, k2, yo, k5, yo, sk2p, yo, k5, yo, sl m, *k2, sl 2, k17; rep from * to next m, k2, sl 2, k9, ssk, k2, sl 2, k2, sl 1 (1 st dec'd)—148 (232) sts rem.

Row 16: P3, sl 2, p12, sl 2, p2, sl m, *p17, sl 2, p2; rep from * to next m, p17, sl 2, p3.

Row 17: Sl 1, C1R, C1L, yo, k1, ssk, p1, k2tog, (k1, yo) two times, k1, ssk, p1, k2tog, k1, yo, sl m, *C1R, C1L, k15; rep from * to next m, C1R, C1L, k6, ssk, C1R, C1L, sl 1 (1 st dec'd).

Row 18: Purl to last m, p3, k1, p7, k1, p10.

Row 19: Sl 1, k2, sl 2, k2, yo, k1, ssk, p1, k2tog, k1, p1, k1, ssk, p1, k2tog, k1, yo, sl m, *k2, sl 2, k17; rep from * to next m, k2, sl 2, k7, ssk, k2, sl 2, k2, sl 1 (1 st dec'd).

Row 20: P3, sl 2, p10, sl 2, p2, sl m, *p17, sl 2, p2; rep from * to next m, p3, (k1, p2) two times, k1, p5, sl 2, p3.

Row 21: Sl 1, C1R, C1L, yo, k1, yo, ssk, p1, k2tog, p1, ssk, p1, k2tog, yo, k1, yo, sl m, *C1R, C1L, k15; rep from * to next m, C1R, C1L, k4, ssk, C1R, C1L, sl 1 (1 st dec'd).

Row 22: Purl to last m, p4, (k1, p1) two times, k1, p11.

Row 23: Sl 1, k2, sl 2, k2, yo, k3, yo, sk2p, p1, k3tog, yo, k3, yo, sl m, *k2, sl 2, k17; rep from * to next m, k2, sl 2, k5, ssk, k2, sl 2, k2, sl 1 (1 st dec'd).

Row 24: P3, sl 2, p8, sl 2, p2, sl m, *p17, sl 2, p2; rep from * to next m, p6, k1, p8, sl 2, p3.

Row 25: Sl 1, C1R, C1L, yo, k5, yo, sk2p, yo, k5, yo, sl m, *C1R, C1L, k15; rep from * to next m, C1R, C1L, k2, ssk, C1R, C1L, sl 1 (1 st dec'd)—143 (227) sts rem.

Row 26: Purl.

Row 27: Sl 1, k2, sl 2, k2, yo, k1, ssk, p1, k2tog, (k1, yo) two times, k1, ssk, p1, k2tog, k1, yo, sl m, *k2, sl 2, k17; rep from * to next m, k2, sl 2, k3, ssk, k2, sl 2, k2, sl 1 (1 st dec'd).

Row 28: P3, sl 2, p6, sl 2, p2, sl m, *p17, sl 2, p2; rep from * to next m, p3, k1, p7, k1, p5, sl 2, p3.

Row 29: Sl 1, C1R, C1L, yo, k1, ssk, p1, k2tog, k1, p1, k1, ssk, p1, k2tog, k1, yo, sl m, *C1R, C1L, k15; rep from * to next m, C1R, C1L, ssk, C1R, C1L, sl 1 (1 st dec'd).

Row 30: Purl to last m, p3, (k1, p2) two times, k1, p10.

Row 31: Sl 1, k2, sl 2, k2, yo, k1, yo, ssk, p1, k2tog, p1, ssk, p1, k2tog, yo, k1, yo, sl m, *k2, sl 2, k17; rep from * to next m, k2, sl 2, k1, ssk, k2, sl 2, k2, sl 1 (1 st dec'd).

Row 32: P3, sl 2, p4, sl 2, p2, sl m, *p17, sl 2, p2; rep from * to next m, p4, (k1, p1) two times, k1, p6, sl 2, p3.

Row 33: Sl 1, C1R, C1L, yo, k3, yo, sk2p, p1, k3tog, yo, k3, yo, sl m, *C1R, C1L, k15; rep from * to next m, C1R, sk2p, C1R, C1L, sl 1 (2 sts dec'd).

Row 34: Purl to last m, p6, k1, p13.

Row 35: Sl 1, k2, sl 2, k2, yo, k5, yo, sk2p, yo, k5, yo, sl m, *k2, sl 2, k17; rep from * to next m, k2, ssk, k2, sl 2, k2, sl 1 (1 st dec'd)—137 (221) sts rem.

Row 36: P3, sl 2, p5, sl m, *p17, sl 2, p2; rep from * to next m, p17, sl 2, p3.

Continue shawl decreases
See also main decrease chart, page 152.

Row 1: (RS) Sl 1, C1R, C1L, yo, k1, ssk, p1, k2tog, (k1, yo) two times, k1, ssk, p1, k2tog, k1, yo, sl m for border, *C1R, C1L, k15; rep from * to patt m, k1, ssk, C1R, C1L, sl 1 (1 st dec'd)—136 (220) sts rem.

Row 2: Purl to last m, p3, k1, p7, k1, p10.

Row 3: Sl 1, k2, sl 2, k2, yo, k1, ssk, p1, k2tog, k1, p1, k1, ssk, p1, k2tog, k1, yo, sl m, *k2, sl 2, k17; rep from * to next m, ssk, k2, sl 2, k2, sl 1 (1 st dec'd).

Row 4 *replace marker:* P3, sl 2, k3, remove patt m, p17, sl 2, p2, pm for patt, *p17, sl 2, p2; rep from * to next m, p3, (k1, p2) two times, k1, p5, sl 2, p3.

Row 5: Sl 1, C1R, C1L, yo, k1, yo, ssk, p1, k2tog, p1, ssk, p1, k2tog, yo, k1, yo, sl m, *C1R, C1L, k15; rep from * to next m, C1R, C1L, k14, ssk, C1R, C1L, sl 1 (1 st dec'd).

Row 6: Purl to last m, p4, (k1, p1) two times, k1, p11.

Row 7: Sl 1, k2, sl 2, k2, yo, k3, yo, sk2p, p1, k3tog, yo, k3, yo, sl m, *k2, sl 2, k17; rep from * to next m, k2, sl 2, k15, ssk, k2, sl 2, k2, sl 1 (1 st dec'd).

Row 8: P3, sl 2, p18, sl 2, p2, sl m, *p17, sl 2, p2; rep from * to next m, p6, k1, p8, sl 2, p3.

Row 9: Sl 1, C1R, C1L, yo, k5, yo, sk2p, yo, k5, yo, sl m, *C1R, C1L, k15; rep from * to next m, C1R, C1L, k12, ssk, C1R, C1L, sl 1 (1 st dec'd)—132 (216) sts rem.

Row 10: Purl.

Row 11: Sl 1, k2, sl 2, k2, yo, k1, ssk, p1, k2tog, (k1, yo) two times, k1, ssk, p1, k2tog, k1, yo, sl m, *k2, sl 2, k17; rep from * to next m, k2, sl 2, k13, ssk, k2, sl 2, k2, sl 1 (1 st dec'd)—131 (215) sts rem.

Row 12: P3, sl 2, p16, sl 2, p2, *p17, sl 2, p2; rep from * to next m, p3, k1, p7, k1, p5, sl 2, p3.

Row 13: Sl 1, C1R, C1L, yo, k1, ssk, p1, k2tog, k1, p1, k1, ssk, p1, k2tog, k1, yo, sl m, *C1R, C1L, k15; rep from * to next m, C1R, C1L, k10, ssk, C1R, C1L, sl 1 (1 st dec'd).

Row 14: Purl to last m, p3, (k1, p2) two times, k1, p10.

Row 15: Sl 1, k2, sl 2, k2, yo, k1, yo, ssk, p1, k2tog, p1, ssk, p1, k2tog, yo, k1, yo, sl m, *k2, sl 2, k17; rep from * to next m, k2, sl 2, k11, ssk, k2, sl 2, k2, sl 1 (1 st dec'd).

Row 16: P3, sl 2, p14, sl 2, p2, sl m, *p17, sl 2, p2; rep from * to next m, p4, (k1, p1) two times, k1, p6, sl 2, p3.

Row 17: Sl 1, C1R, C1L, yo, k3, yo, sk2p, p1, k3tog, yo, k3, yo, sl m, *C1R, C1L, k15; rep from * to next m, C1R, C1L, k8, ssk, C1R, C1L, sl 1 (1 st dec'd).

Row 18: Purl to last m, p6, k1, p13.

Row 19: Sl 1, k2, sl 2, k2, yo, k5, yo, sk2p, yo, k5, yo, sl m, *k2, sl 2, k17; rep from * to next m, k2, sl 2, k9, ssk, k2, sl 2, k2, sl 1 (1 st dec'd)—127 (211) sts rem.

Row 20: P3, sl 2, p12, sl 2, p2, sl m, *p17, sl 2, p2; rep from * to next m, p17, sl 2, p3.

Row 21: Sl 1, C1R, C1L, yo, k1, ssk, p1, k2tog, (k1, yo) two times, k1, ssk, p1, k2tog, k1, yo, sl m, *C1R, C1L, k15; rep from * to next m, C1R, C1L, k6, ssk, C1R, C1L, sl 1 (1 st dec'd)—126 (210) sts rem.

Row 22: Purl to last m, p3, k1, p7, k1, p10.

Row 23: Sl 1, k2, sl 2, k2, yo, k1, ssk, p1, k2tog, k1, p1, k1, ssk, p1, k2tog, k1, yo, sl m, *k2, sl 2, k17; rep from * to next m, k2, sl 2, k7, ssk, k2, sl 2, k2, sl 1 (1 st dec'd).

Row 24: P3, sl 2, p10, sl 2, p2, sl m, *p17, sl 2, p2; rep from * to next m, p3, (k1, p2) two times, k1, p5, sl 2, p3.

Row 25: Sl 1, C1R, C1L, yo, k1, yo, ssk, p1, k2tog, p1, ssk, p1, k2tog, yo, k1, yo, sl m, *C1R, C1L, k15; rep from * to next m, C1R, C1L, k4, ssk, C1R, C1L, sl 1 (1 st dec'd).

Row 26: Purl to last m, p4, (k1, p1) two times, k1, p11.

Row 27: Sl 1, k2, sl 2, k2, yo, k3, yo, sk2p, p1, k3tog, yo, k3, yo, sl m, *k2, sl 2, k17; rep from * to next m, k2, sl 2, k5, ssk, k2, sl 2, k2, sl 1 (1 st dec'd).

Row 28: P3, sl 2, p8, sl 2, p2, sl m, *p17, sl 2, p2; rep from * to next m, p6, k1, p8, sl 2, p3.

Row 29: Sl 1, C1R, C1L, yo, k5, yo, sk2p, yo, k5, yo, sl m, *C1R, C1L, k15; rep from * to next m, C1R, C1L, k2, ssk, C1R, C1L, sl 1 (1 st dec'd)—122 (206) sts rem.

Row 30: Purl.

Row 31: Sl 1, k2, sl 2, k2, yo, k1, ssk, p1, k2tog, (k1, yo) two times, k1, ssk, p1, k2tog, k1, yo, sl m, *k2, sl 2, k17; rep from * to next m, k2, sl 2, k3, ssk, k2, sl 2, k2, sl 1 (1 st dec'd)—121 (205) sts rem.

Row 32: P3, sl 2, p6, sl 2, p2, sl m, *p17, sl 2, p2; rep from * to next m, p3, k1, p7, k1, p5, sl 2, p3.

Row 33: Sl 1, C1R, C1L, yo, k1, ssk, p1, k2tog, k1, p1, k1, ssk, p1, k2tog, k1, yo, sl m, *C1R, C1L, k15; rep from * to next m, C1R, C1L, ssk, C1R, C1L, sl 1 (1 st dec'd).

Row 34: Purl to last m, p3, (k1, p2) two times, k1, p10.

Row 35: Sl 1, k2, sl 2, k2, yo, k1, yo, ssk, p1, k2tog, p1, ssk, p1, k2tog, yo, k1, yo, sl m, *k2, sl 2, k17; rep from * to next m, k2, sl 2, k1, ssk, k2, sl 2, k2, sl 1 (1 st dec'd).

Row 36: P3, sl 2, p4, sl 2, p2, sl m, *p17, sl 2, p2; rep from * to next m, p4, (k1, p1) two times, k1, p6, sl 2, p3.

Row 37: Sl 1, C1R, C1L, yo, k3, yo, sk2p, p1, k3tog, yo, k3, yo, sl m, *C1R, C1L, k15; rep from * to next m, C1R, sk2p, C1R, C1L, sl 1 (2 sts dec'd).

Row 38: Purl to last m, p6, k1, p13.

Row 39: Sl 1, k2, sl 2, k2, yo, k5, yo, sk2p, yo, k5, yo, sl m, *k2, sl 2, k17; rep from * to next m, k2, ssk, k2, sl 2, k2, sl 1 (1 st dec'd)—116 (200) sts rem.

Row 40: P3, sl 2, p5, sl m, *p17, sl 2, p2; rep from * to next m, p17, sl 2, p3.

Rep the last 40 rows 2 (6) more times—74 sts rem.

Work Rows 1-40 one more time, working pattern repeat one time between markers after Row 4, and removing markers on the final row—53 sts rem.

Continue shawl decreases

See also final decrease chart, page 153.

Row 1: (RS) Sl 1, C1R, C1L, yo, k1, ssk, p1, k2tog, (k1, yo) two times, k1, ssk, p1, k2tog, k1, yo, C1R, C1L, k16, ssk, C1R, C1L, sl 1 (1 st dec'd)—52 sts rem.

Row 2: Purl to last 19 sts, k1, p7, k1, p10.

Row 3: Sl 1, k2, sl 2, k2, yo, k1, ssk, p1, k2tog, k1, p1, k1, ssk, p1, k2tog, k1, yo, k2, sl 2, k17, ssk, k2, sl 2, k2, sl 1 (1 st dec'd).

Row 4: P3, sl 2, p20, sl 2, p5, (k1, p2) two times, k1, p5, sl 2, p3.

Row 5: Sl 1, C1R, C1L, yo, k1, yo, ssk, p1, k2tog, p1, ssk, p1, k2tog, yo, k1, yo, C1R, C1L, k14, ssk, C1R, C1L, sl 1 (1 st dec'd).

Row 6: Purl to last 16 sts, (k1, p1) two times, k1, p11.

Row 7: Sl 1, k2, sl 2, k2, yo, k3, yo, sk2p, p1, k3tog, yo, k3, yo, k2, sl 2, k15, ssk, k2, sl 2, k2, sl 1 (1 st dec'd).

Row 8: P3, sl 2, p18, sl 2, p8, k1, p8, sl 2, p3.

Row 9: Sl 1, C1R, C1L, yo, k5, yo, sk2p, yo, k5, yo, C1R, C1L, k12, ssk, C1R, C1L, sl 1 (1 st dec'd)—48 sts rem.

Row 10: Purl.

Row 11: Sl 1, k2, sl 2, k2, yo, k1, ssk, p1, k2tog, (k1, yo) two times, k1, ssk, p1, k2tog, k1, yo, k2, sl 2, k13, ssk, k2, sl 2, k2, sl 1 (1 st dec'd)—47 sts rem.

Row 12: P3, sl 2, p16, sl 2, p5, k1, p7, k1, p5, sl 2, p3.

Row 13: Sl 1, C1R, C1L, yo, k1, ssk, p1, k2tog, k1, p1, k1, ssk, p1, k2tog, k1, yo, C1R, C1L, k10, ssk, C1R, C1L, sl 1 (1 st dec'd).

Row 14: Purl to last 17 sts, (k1, p2) two times, k1, p10.

Row 15: Sl 1, k2, sl 2, k2, yo, k1, yo, ssk, p1, k2tog, p1, ssk, p1, k2tog, yo, k1, yo, k2, sl 2, k11, ssk, k2, sl 2, k2, sl 1 (1 st dec'd).

Row 16: P3, sl 2, p14, sl 2, p6, (k1, p1) two times, k1, p6, sl 2, p3.

Row 17: Sl 1, C1R, C1L, yo, k3, yo, sk2p, p1, k3tog, yo, k3, yo, C1R, C1L, k8, ssk, C1R, C1L, sl 1 (1 st dec'd).

Row 18: Purl to last 14 sts, k1, p13.

Row 19: Sl 1, k2, sl 2, k2, yo, k5, yo, sk2p, yo, k5, yo, k2, sl 2, k9, ssk, k2, sl 2, k2, sl 1 (1 st dec'd)—43 sts rem.

Row 20: P3, sl 2, p12, sl 2, p19, sl 2, p3.

Row 21: Sl 1, C1R, C1L, yo, k1, ssk, p1, k2tog, (k1, yo) two times, k1, ssk, p1, k2tog, k1, yo, C1R, C1L, k6, ssk, C1R, C1L, sl 1 (1 st dec'd)—42 sts rem.

Row 22: Purl to last 19 sts, k1, p7, k1, p10.

Row 23: Sl 1, k2, sl 2, k2, yo, k1, ssk, p1, k2tog, k1, p1, k1, ssk, p1, k2tog, k1, yo, k2, sl 2, k7, ssk, k2, sl 2, k2, sl 1 (1 st dec'd).

Row 24: P3, sl 2, p10, sl 2, p5, (k1, p2) two times, k1, p5, sl 2, p3.

Row 25: Sl 1, C1R, C1L, yo, k1, yo, ssk, p1, k2tog, p1, ssk, p1, k2tog, yo, k1, yo, C1R, C1L, k4, ssk, C1R, C1L, sl 1 (1 st dec'd).

Row 26: Purl to last 16 sts, (k1, p1) two times, k1, p11.

Row 27: Sl 1, k2, sl 2, k2, yo, k3, yo, sk2p, p1, k3tog, yo, k3, yo, k2, sl 2, k5, ssk, k2, sl 2, k2, sl 1 (1 st dec'd).

Row 28: P3, sl 2, p8, sl 2, p8, k1, p8, sl 2, p3.

Row 29: Sl 1, C1R, C1L, yo, k5, yo, sk2p, yo, k5, yo, C1R, C1L, k2, ssk, C1R, C1L, sl 1 (1 st dec'd)—38 sts rem.

Row 30: Purl.

Row 31: Sl 1, k2, sl 2, k2, yo, k1, ssk, p1, k2tog, (k1, yo) two times, k1, ssk, p1, k2tog, k1, yo, k2, sl 2, k3, ssk, k2, sl 2, k2, sl 1 (1 st dec'd)—37 sts rem.

Row 32: P3, sl 2, p6, sl 2, p5, k1, p7, k1, p5, sl 2, p3.

Row 33: Sl 1, C1R, C1L, yo, k1, ssk, p1, k2tog, k1, p1, k1, ssk, p1, k2tog, k1, yo, C1R, C1L, ssk, C1R, C1L, sl 1 (1 st dec'd).

Row 34: P17, (k1, p2) two times, k1, p10.

Row 35: Sl 1, k2, sl 2, k2, yo, k1, yo, ssk, p1, k2tog, p1, ssk, p1, k2tog, yo, k1, yo, k2, sl 2, k1, ssk, k2, sl 2, k2, sl 1 (1 st dec'd).

Row 36: P3, sl 2, p4, sl 2, p6, (k1, p1) two times, k1, p6, sl 2, p3.

Row 37: Sl 1, C1R, C1L, yo, k3, yo, sk2p, p1, k3tog, yo, k3, yo, C1R, sk2p, C1R, C1L, sl 1 (2 sts dec'd).
Row 38: P17, k1, p13.
Row 39: Sl 1, k2, sl 2, k2, yo, k5, yo, sk2p, yo, k5, yo, k2, ssk, k2, sl 2, k2, sl 1 (1 st dec'd)—32 sts rem.
Row 40: P3, sl 2, purl to last 5 sts, sl 2, p3.

Begin final decreases

See also shawl end chart, page 153.

Row 1: (RS) Sl 1, C1R, C1L, yo, k1, ssk, p1, k2tog, (k1, yo) two times, k1, ssk, p1, k2tog, k1, yo, k1, ssk, C1R, C1L, sl 1 (1 st dec'd)—31 sts rem.
Row 2: P12, k1, p7, k1, p10.
Row 3: Sl 1, k2, sl 2, k2, yo, k1, ssk, p1, k2tog, k1, p1, k1, ssk, p1, k2tog, k1, yo, ssk, k2, sl 2, k2, sl 1 (3 sts dec'd)—28 sts rem.
Row 4: P3, sl 2, p6, (k1, p2) two times, k1, p5, sl 2, p3.
Row 5: Sl 1, C1R, C1L, k1, yo, ssk, p1, k2tog, p1, ssk, p1, k2tog, yo, ssk, C1R, C1L, sl 1 (3 sts dec'd)—25 sts rem.
Row 6: P10, (k1, p1) two times, k1, p10.
Row 7: Sl 1, k2, sl 2, k2, k2tog, yo, sk2p, p1, k3tog, yo, ssk, k2, sl 2, k2, sl 1 (4 sts dec'd)—21 sts rem.
Row 8: P3, sl 2, p5, k1, p5, sl 2, p3.
Row 9: Sl 1, C1R, C1L, k2tog, yo, sk2p, yo, ssk, C1R, C1L, sl 1 (2 sts dec'd)—19 sts rem.
Row 10: Purl.
Row 11: Sl 1, k2, sl 2, k3, sk2p, k3, sl 2, k2, sl 1 (2 sts dec'd)—17 sts rem.
Row 12: P3, sl 2, p7, sl 2, p3.
Row 13: Sl 1, C1R, C1L, sk2p, C1R, C1L, sl 1 (2 sts dec'd)—15 sts rem.
Row 14: Purl.
Row 15: Sl 1, k2, sl 2, k1, ssk, k2, sl 2, k2, sl 1 (1 st dec'd)—14 sts rem.

Row 16: P3, sl 2, p4, sl 2, p3.
Row 17: Sl 1, C1R, sk2p, C1R, C1L, sl 1 (2 sts dec'd)—12 sts rem.
Row 18: Purl.
Row 19: Sl 1, k1, sk2p, k2, sl 2, k2, sl 1 (2 sts dec'd)—10 sts rem.
Row 20: P3, sl 2, p5.
Row 21: Sk2p, k3tog, sk2p, sl 1 (6 sts dec'd)—4 sts rem.
Next row: (WS) Bind off purlwise.

Finishing

Weave in ends. Wet block shawl to finished measurements.

BORDER PATTERN

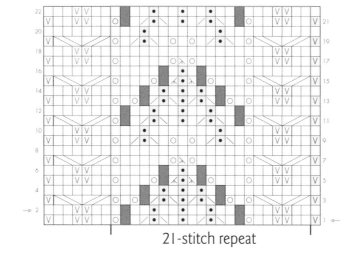

21-stitch repeat

KEY

knit on RS, purl on WS

purl on RS, knit on WS

V sl 1 knitwise with yarn to WS

V sl 1 purlwise with yarn to WS

O yo

p1-tbl on WS

k2tog

ssk

k3tog

sk2p

C1R [see Special abbreviations]

C1L [see Special abbreviations]

no stitch

pattern repeat

border marker

pattern marker

SET UP PATTERN

pattern marker

border marker

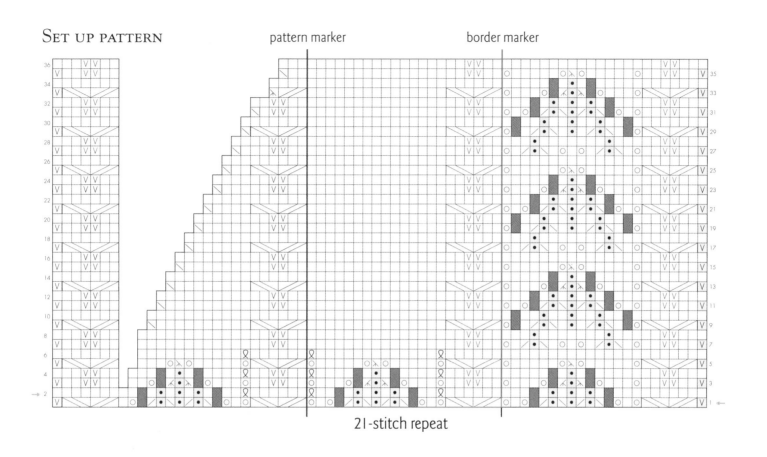

21-stitch repeat

Main decrease pattern

pattern marker

border marker

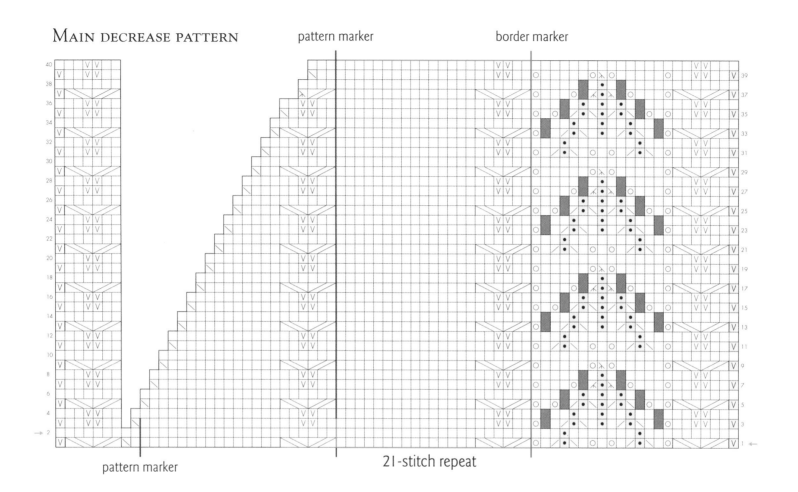

pattern marker

21-stitch repeat

FINAL DECREASE PATTERN

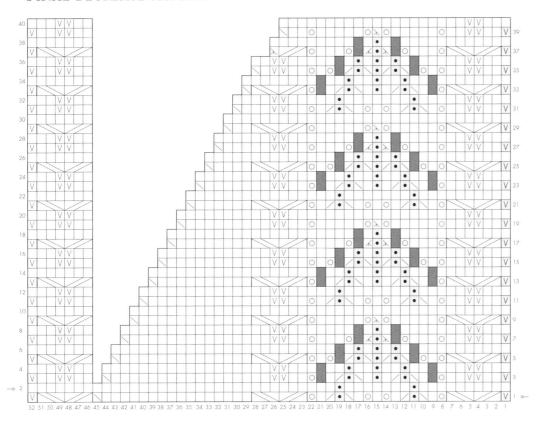

SHAWL END

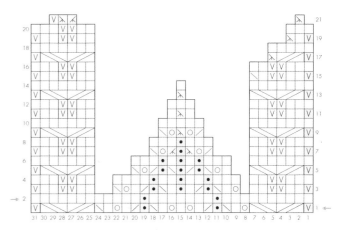

Resources

stockinette stitch (St st)
Knit on the RS, purl on the WS.

garter stitch
Knit every row.

For great illustrated tutorials on the following techniques, visit our blog, quinceandco.com/blogs/news/tagged/techniques

long-tail cast on

picking up stitches

cabling without a cable needle

yarnover short rows

STANDARD ABBREVIATIONS

beg	begin(ning); begin(s)
BO	bind off
CO	cast on
circ	circular needle
cm	centimeter(s)
cn	cable needle
cont	continue(s); continuing
dec('d)	decrease(d)
est	establish(ed)
g	gram(s)
inc('d)	increase(d)
k	knit
LH	left hand
mm	millimeter(s)
m	marker(s)
mult	multiple
p	purl
patt(s)	pattern(s)
pm	place marker
rem	remain(ing); remain(s)
rep	repeat(ing); repeat(s)
RH	right hand
rib	ribbing
RS	right side
sl	slip
sl m	slip marker
st(s)	stitch(es)
St st	stockinette stitch
tbl	through the back loop
tog	together
WS	wrong side
yd	yard(s)

SPECIAL ABBREVIATIONS

k1-f/b (knit 1, front and back): Knit into the front loop, then the back loop of next stitch (1 stitch increased).

k1-tbl: Knit 1 stitch through the back loop to twist stitch.

k2tog: Knit 2 stitches together (1 stitch decreased, leans to the right).

k2tog-tbl: Knit 2 stitches together through the back loops (1 stitch decreased).

k3tog: Knit 3 stitches together (2 stitches decreased, leans to the right).

m1-p/L (make 1 purlwise left slanting): Insert LH needle from front to back under horizontal strand between stitch just worked and next stitch, purl lifted strand through the back loop (1 stitch increased).

m1-p/R (make 1 purlwise right slanting): Insert LH needle from back to front under horizontal strand between stitch just worked and next stitch, purl lifted strand through the front loop (1 stitch increased).

M1L (make 1 left slanting): Insert LH needle from front to back under horizontal strand between stitch just worked and next stitch, knit lifted strand through the back loop (1 stitch increased).

M1R (make 1 right slanting): Insert LH needle from back to front under horizontal strand between stitch just worked and next stitch, knit lifted strand through the front loop (1 stitch increased).

p1-tbl: Purl 1 stitch through the back loop to twist stitch.

p2tog: Purl 2 stitches together (1 stitch decreased).

p2tog-tbl: Purl 2 stitches together through the back loops (1 stitch decreased).

p3tog: Purl 3 stitches together (2 stitches decreased).

s2kp (central double decrease): Slip 2 stitches tog knitwise to the RH needle, k1, pass 2 slipped stitches over knit stitch (2 stitches decreased).

sk2p: Slip 1 stitch knitwise to RH needle, k2tog, pass slipped stitch over stitch created by k2tog (2 stitches decreased, leans to the left).

ssk (slip, slip, knit): Slip 2 stitches one at a time knitwise to the RH needle; return stitches to LH needle in turned position and knit them together through the back loops (1 stitch decreased, leans to the left).

ssp (slip, slip, purl): Slip 2 stitches one at a time knitwise to the RH needle; return stitches to LH needle in turned position and purl them together through the back loops (1 stitch decreased).

sssk (slip, slip, slip, knit): Slip 3 stitches one at a time knitwise to the RH needle; return stitches to LH needle in turned position and knit them together through the back loops (2 stitches decreased, leans to the left).

yo (yarn over): (1 stitch increased)

Between 2 knit stitches: Bring yarn between needles to the front, then over RH needle ready to knit the next stitch.

Between a knit and a purl stitch: Bring yarn between needles to the front, over RH needle, then between needles to front again, ready to purl the next stitch.

Between 2 purl stitches: Bring yarn over RH needle, then between needles to the front, ready to purl the next stitch.

Between a purl and a knit stitch: Bring yarn over the RH needle, ready to knit the next stitch.

HISTORY & BIO

Quince & Co is a handknitting yarn and knitwear design company launched in 2010 by Pam Allen in partnership with a historic spinning mill in Maine. Our goal is to work as much as possible with American fibers and mills and, when we can't have a yarn made to our specifications in the US, we look for suppliers overseas who make yarn in as earth- and labor-friendly a way as possible.

Quince began with a core line of five wool yarns—Finch, Chickadee, Lark, Osprey, and Puffin—each with its own personality, each in 37 colors, and all spun in the US from American wool. Today Quince & Co's core line comes in more than 60 colors and we've added Tern, a silk/wool blend, Owl, an alpaca/wool blend, Piper and Crane, two super fine mohair/merino blends, Willet and Whimbrel, two cotton yarns sourced from a Cleaner Cotton™ grower in California, and Phoebe, a super soft merino yarn. In addition, Quince makes two organic linen yarns, Sparrow and Kestrel, with a mill in Italy. Find out more at www.quinceandco.com.

Leila Raven began knitting on a whim in 2003 and never looked back.

ACKNOWLEDGEMENTS

Photography by Leila Raven
Modeling by Judith Davis
Illustrations by Leila Raven
Production by Dawn Catanzaro, Jerusha Neely, Hallie Ojala-Barrett
Sample knitting by Dawn Catanzaro, Karin Mueller, Adi Kehoe, Hallie Ojala-Barrett, Jerusha Neely
Pattern testing by Aleisha F, Ali R, Ana C, Barb C, Bethany H, Bri R, Christina G, Christine P, Danielle B, Elisabeth B, Elizabeth S, Fay W, Frances S, Glenna E, Ingrid C, Jeanette B, Jen D, Josephine C, Kamilla K, Kelly K, Kimberley B, Kylie I, Linda P, Liz H, Marylyn S, Melissa G, Melissa N, Mia M, Nathalie M, Nicole C, Salena K, Sarah L, Shauna M, Sue H, Suzanne W, Terri H, Yvonne M

Our gratitude to Laurel Noyes for opening her North Berwick, ME, home to us for our shoot.

Extra special thanks to Dawn—my friend, you are seen, you are heard, you are loved.

NOTES